Walking With Purpose · Young Adult Bible Studies

GOD'S LOVE IN THREE-PART HARMONY

Walking with the Lord is a journey that lasts a lifetime. If you enjoyed the *Opening Your Heart Series*, look out for these new Bible studies that will continue to nurture your soul.

THE KEEPING IN BALANCE SERIES

Harmony – Part I
How to find the balance between mediocrity and perfectionism and become the woman God created you to be without stressing.

Perspective – Part II
Become more content and grow stronger in the face of failure, and keep moving when you're tempted to settle for the status quo.

Exhale – Part III
Ideas for establishing a rhythm of rest, worship, and surrender and reorder your thoughts to create inner peace.

THE DISCOVERING OUR DIGNITY SERIES

Tapestry – Part I
From relationship challenges, to the death of dreams, and the lure of compromise– how to apply age-old wisdom from the women of Genesis to the challenges of today.

Legacy – Part II
Explore a myriad of women's issues such as shame, loneliness, and making a difference in the world, and learn from the wisdom of ancient women.

Heritage – Part III
Inspiration about work and worship from key women in the New Testament, including Mary, the Blessed Mother, and her insights on what it means to live sacrificially.

For more spiritual inspiration or to learn more about Walking With Purpose, visit us at walkingwithpurpose.com

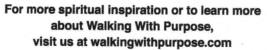

walking with purpose

You're also invited to join our community on Facebook, Twitter, Pinterest and Instagram.

Dear friend,

Welcome to *Perspective*, part II of the *Keeping in Balance* young adult Bible study series! Thank you for delving into God's Word with me. I know that there are countless ways you can pursue personal growth, better balance and spiritual maturity. The fact that you are willing to give this Bible study a try means the world to me.

We're all being influenced every day, hour by hour, minute by minute. It's been said that everyone worships something– that's the thing we're willing to sacrifice for. You get to choose what (or who) you worship. Worshipping God and becoming more like Jesus doesn't just happen automatically– it occurs when a woman decides that she wants to be influenced by God more than the culture, or others' expectations or her own desires. Discipleship happens when you answer the call to follow Jesus and let Him shape you.

But along this road, obstacles are inevitable. Doubt collides with faith, weariness gets in the way of perseverance, and the temptation to water down the gospel pulls us toward compromise. The best defense and offense comes by learning to wield the sword of the Spirit– the Word of God (Eph. 6:17). You'll grow in your ability to do this as you move through the pages of this study.

God is meeting you right where you are. He is encouraging you to shift your perspective from your feelings, circumstances and fears, and place them instead on the eternal truths He has revealed. Bring your angst, wrestling, and unsettled thoughts to Him. There is nothing He can't handle. But approach with an open heart, and a desire to build a life that needs God. That thing which you think disqualifies you? It's the place where you need God most. And never forget, God's power is made perfect in weakness (2 Corinth. 12:9).

Praying we'll fix our eyes on Jesus,
Lisa Brenninkmeyer
Founder and Chief Purpose Officer of Walking with Purpose

Perspective
Keeping in Balance Series
Part II

www.walkingwithpurpose.com

Authored by Lisa Brenninkmeyer
Cover and page design by True Cotton
Production management by Christine Welsko

IMPRIMATUR + William E. Lori, S.T.D., Archbishop of Baltimore

The recommended Bible translations for use in Blaze and Walking with Purpose studies are: The New American Bible, which is the translation used in the United States for the readings at Mass; The Revised Standard Version, Catholic Edition; and The Jerusalem Bible.

Any internet addresses (websites, blogs, etc.) in this book are offered as a resource and may change in the future. Please refer to www.walkingwithpurpose.com as the central location for corresponding materials and references.

The New Church Lady," *Pearls and Grace* (blog), February 6, 2014, is reprinted with permission from author/ speaker Sibi Riffer.

Printed: November 2018

ISBN: 978-1-943173-23-5

Keeping in Balance Series, Part II

TABLE OF CONTENTS

INTRODUCTION

LESSONS

APPENDICES

ANSWER KEY

PRAYER PAGES

NOTES

Welcome to Walking with Purpose

You have many choices when it comes to how you spend your time—thank you for choosing Walking with Purpose. Studying God's Word with an open and receptive heart will bring spiritual growth and enrichment to all aspects of your life, making every moment that you've invested well worth it.

Each one of us comes to this material from our own unique vantage point. You are welcome as you are. No previous experience is necessary. Some of you will find that the questions in this study cause you to think about concepts that are new to you. Others might find much is a review. God meets each one of us where we are, and He is always faithful, taking us to a deeper, better place spiritually, regardless of where we begin.

The Structure of *Keeping in Balance* Series

The *Keeping in Balance* series is a three-part Bible study, each of which can stand alone, or all three can be completed one after the other. Each Bible study integrates Scripture with the teachings of the Roman Catholic Church to point us to principles that help us manage life's pace and pressure while living with calm and steadiness.

This Bible study can be used on your own, giving you great material for daily Scripture meditation and prayer. It also lends itself well to group discussion. We encourage you to gather your tribe—a handful of friends who want more out of their spiritual lives. The accountability and deeper friendship that will result make it so much easier to live out the truths contained in these pages.

Study Guide Format and Reference Materials

The three parts of *Perspective - Keeping in Balance Part II* are divided into three sections:

The first section comprises five lessons, which are divided into five "days" to help you form a habit of reading and reflecting on God's Word regularly. If you are a young woman who has only bits and pieces of time throughout your day to

3

accomplish tasks, you will find this breakdown of the lessons especially helpful. Each day focuses on Scripture readings and related teaching passages, and ends with a Quiet Your Heart reflection, which should lead you to a time of personal prayer. In addition, Day Five includes a Saint's Story; a lesson conclusion; a resolution section, in which you set a goal for yourself based on a theme of the lesson; and short clips from the *Catechism of the Catholic Church*, which are referenced throughout the lesson to complement the Scripture study.

The second section, the appendices, contains supplemental materials referred to during the study.

The third section contains the answer key. You will benefit so much more from the Bible study if you work through the questions on your own, searching your heart, as this is your very personal journey of faith. The answer key is meant to enhance small group discussion and provide personal guidance or insight when needed.

A memory verse has been chosen for each part of the *Keeping in Balance* series, and we encourage you to memorize it as you move through the Bible study. An illustration of the verse can be found in the Introduction section, and a color version and phone lock screen can be downloaded from our website.

At the end of the book are pages on which to write weekly prayer intentions.

Walking with Purpose™ Young Adult Bible Studies

The *Opening Your Heart* Series

Beloved: *Opening Your Heart, Part I* is a six-lesson Bible study that lays a strong foundation for our true identity as beloved daughters of God. We'll learn that we belong to a family that will never abandon us. We'll encounter grace and practical tools to make God our first priority. Jesus will meet us personally in the pages of His Word, and we'll be transformed as a result.

Unshaken: *Opening Your Heart, Part II* is a six-lesson Bible study that fills our spiritual toolbox with exactly what we need to grow stronger in our faith. We'll discuss why and how we should read the Bible, what difference the sacraments really make in our lives, how to bravely face challenges in our efforts to follow Christ, and the way Mary perfectly mothers us through it all.

Steadfast: *Opening Your Heart, Part III,* a six-lesson Bible study, unpacks why we are hustling for our worth and how to conquer our fears. We'll look at the role of suffering and forgiveness in our lives, and dig deeper into how we can truly change in the areas where we have felt enslaved. We'll explore life purpose, our vocations, and the depth of God's personal love for His beloved children.

The *Keeping in Balance* Series

Harmony: *Keeping in Balance, Part I* is a five-lesson Bible study that helps us to get a grip on our lives by looking at the importance of authenticity, setting priorities, managing expectations, and having healthy relationships. We'll also explore finding a balance between mediocrity and perfectionism so that we can become the women God created us to be without stressing or striving.

Perspective: *Keeping in Balance, Part II* is a five-lesson Bible study that addresses how we can become more content, grow stronger in areas where we've failed a million times, and get moving when we feel like settling for the status quo. *Perspective* also explores how we can engage our culture as Catholics at a time when the reputation of Christians is at an all-time low.

Exhale: *Keeping in Balance, Part III* is a six-lesson Bible study that helps us establish a rhythm of rest, worship, and surrender. If you long for more simplicity in your life and are ready to order your thoughts so you can experience inner peace, this Bible study will both inspire you and provide you with practical steps to make positive changes.

The *Discovering Our Dignity* Series: *Coming Soon*

Tapestry: *Discovering Our Dignity, Part I* is a six-lesson Bible study that explores the beginning of salvation history through the eyes of the women of Genesis. The difficulties they struggled with are remarkably similar to our own: relationship challenges, the death of dreams, the lure of compromise, and the danger of self-reliance. We'll learn from their mistakes as we apply age-old wisdom to our modern challenges.

Legacy: *Discovering Our Dignity, Part II* is a nine-lesson Bible study that picks up where *Tapestry* left off. Our exploration of the women of salvation history continues as we move further into the Old Testament. We'll explore a myriad of women's issues such as loneliness, shame, leadership challenges, and making a difference in the world.

Heritage: *Discovering Our Dignity, Part III* is a seven-lesson Bible Study that highlights key women of the New Testament. Mary and Martha will help us explore the balance of work and worship, and the poor widow will shed new light on what it means to live sacrificially. We'll be inspired especially by Mary, the Blessed Mother, as we apply her wisdom to our daily challenges.

take every thought captive in OBEDIENCE to Christ

2 corinthians 10:5

walking with purpose

[1] Full-Color Free Printables available at walkingwithpurpose.com/free-printables

Walking with Purpose™ Website

Please visit our website at www.walkingwithpurpose.com to find supplemental materials that complement our Bible studies; a link to our online store for additional Bible studies, DVDs, books, and more; and the following free content:

WWP Scripture Printables of our exclusively designed verse cards that complement all Bible studies. Available in various sizes, lock screens for phones, and a format that allows you to e-mail them to friends.

WWP Bible Study Playlists of Lisa's favorite music to accompany each Bible study.

WWP Videos of all Connect Coffee Talks by Lisa Brenninkmeyer.

WWP Blog by Lisa Brenninkmeyer, a safe place where you are welcome, where the mask can drop and you can be real. Subscribe for updates.

WWP Leadership Development Program

We are here to help you take your leadership to the next level! Through our training, you'll discover insights that help you achieve your leadership potential. You'll be empowered to step out of your comfort zone and experience the rush of serving God with passion and purpose. We want you to know that you are not alone; we offer you encouragement and the tools you need to reach out to a world that desperately needs to experience the love of God.

Links to WWP Social Media

Twitter, Pinterest, Facebook, Instagram

Lessons

NOTES

Lesson 1

BALANCE THROUGH SERVICE

Introduction

In his book, *A Hidden Wholeness*, Parker Palmer tells a story about farmers in the Midwest who would prepare for blizzards by tying a rope to the back door of their house out to the barn as a guide so that they could be sure they could get home again. With a blizzard swirling, visibility was nonexistent, and without a rope to guide you, it was possible to never find your door, even if you were only feet from it.[2]

Many of us have lost our way in the whiteout of the blizzard swirling around us. Blizzards begin when we say yes to too many things. We multitask so much that we don't even notice that we are doing three things at once. We admire people who are able to do so much in so little time. They are our role models.

God desires that His daughters learn to rest. We aren't workhorses, valued for what we produce. As children of God, we need to live in the rhythm He designed for us. But in our desire to rest, we can also go to the other extreme. We can live for comfort, always pursuing the easiest route. An example of this was shared in the British periodical *The Week*:

> Wealthy Americans have found a cunning way of jumping the queues at Disney World: they simply hire a disabled person to act as their "tour concierge." For $130 an hour, the "concierges" pose as a family member, using their disability privileges to get the whole group straight onto rides. "This is how the 1% does Disney," said one member of Manhattan's financial elite.[3]

---

[2] Parker Palmer, *A Hidden Wholeness* (San Francisco, CA: Jossey Bass- A Wiley Imprint, 2004), 1.

[3] "This Year, in the Tabloids," *The Week*, December 18, 2013.

Granted, most of us would never go to these lengths to take the easy route. But the truth is, the desire to stay cozy and comfortable, taking what we can get and complaining about how busy and tired we are, is pretty strong. God calls us to be other-focused. We are to rest so that we are reenergized to be His hands and feet in a world that is in desperate need of the touch of the Savior.

What do you see in the world that is not right? What gets you off the couch saying, "Somebody has got to do something about that!" Could it be that the somebody God is calling to step out and bring change is you?

Is the problem you see an enormous one? Don't let the size of the mess or the injustice deter you. God doesn't ask you to solve the whole thing. He asks you to do your part. And all our parts put together—if only we'd be obedient to His call on our hearts—would render the world unrecognizable.

"We know only too well that what we are doing is nothing more than a drop in the ocean. But if the drop were not there, the ocean would be missing something."
—Saint Teresa of Calcutta

Day One
DON'T HOLD BACK

Read Matthew 25:14–30, CCC 1936, and CCC 1937.

1. Regardless of who was handling the talents at a particular moment, whom did they belong to? Who was to benefit from the investment of the talents?

2. Jesus is the master of this parable, and we are the servants. Each of us has been given talents, which we are to use to advance *Christ's* kingdom and purposes, not our own. What happens on a local and global scale when Christians ignore this truth? See CCC 1936 and CCC 1937.

3. Why did the lazy servant bury his talent in the ground? What do you think was his concept of his master? Can you see any parallels between the lazy servant's reason for burying his talent and reasons why we might hold back from serving God?

4. What would change in your life if you put all your talents directly at the service of Christ the King? What would change in your home? Your neighborhood? Your parish?

In his book *The Better Part*, Father John Bartunek challenges us to expand our perspective on the breadth of the talents God has entrusted to us:

> Note secondly what the Church has always understood by talents: every gift we have received from God, starting with the gift of existence, including all the capabilities of our bodies and minds, extending to education, culture, faith, the sacraments, vocation, and every opportunity and resource without our personal sphere of influence—from money to artistic sensibility, from creative genius to physical prowess, from freedom of speech to the elusive entity of time itself. In other words, we have received everything from God, and we are free either to take all our gifts and squander them, burying them in the hole of self-indulgence, fear, laziness, and greed . . . or to give them back to God by putting them to work for his Kingdom. Nothing escapes the eternal reckoning, so everything is a chance to build up or tear down our relationship with God. In

this parable, Christ implores us: "Live for the things that last! . . . Don't be afraid to lay everything on the line for me and for the Church!"[4]

Quiet your heart and enjoy His presence. . . . Let His blessings fill your heart, then let them overflow to others.

Father John Bartunek writes the following to encourage us to offer God our talents for the sake of His kingdom. He imagines Jesus' pain when we keep them for ourselves out of indifference, resentment, or fear:

> *Jesus: I created you to know me and love me, to live in my friendship now and for all eternity. I have limited my omnipotence in giving you this possibility, because friendship requires freedom, and freedom necessitates the possibility that you will reject my friendship. But you have nothing to fear from me, nothing to lose in following me. You gain everything by accepting my invitation. Enjoy the life and talents I have given you, invest them for eternity, and trust that I will never demand from you more than you are capable of giving.*[5]

Take a few moments to talk to Jesus about the talents He's given you. Ask Him to lift any blindness that is keeping you from seeing how He has uniquely gifted you. When He gave out talents, He did not skip you. Every single one of His daughters has been equipped with spiritual gifts— you included.

Even when we recognize that God is calling us to serve Him in our broken world, certain barriers can hold us back from stepping out, or tempt us to quit once we've gotten started. The following four days will explore some of the things that keep us from setting out and living the purposeful, fulfilling life that comes with serving Christ wholeheartedly with all we've got.

Day Two
THINKING IT HAS TO BE HUGE

Read Luke 10:25–37.

One of the barriers to serving the Lord is our sense that for it to be worth it, we have to do some far-reaching, noteworthy task. As a result, we delay. We tell ourselves that

---

[4] Father John Bartunek, *The Better Part: A Christ-Centered Resource for Personal Prayer* (Hamden, CT: Circle Press, 2007), 292.

[5] Ibid, 293.

we haven't said no to God, we're just waiting for the right opportunity to come along. Or perhaps we see the copious need in the world, and doubt that the little bit we could do would make much difference.

Theophan the Recluse, desiring to challenge and comfort a woman who was searching for purpose, wrote the following:

> I would guess that among your friends are progressive thinkers. . . . The progressives have in mind all mankind or at least all of its people lumped together. The fact is, however, that "mankind" or "the people" does not exist as a person for whom you could do something right now. It consists of individual persons; by doing something for one person, we are doing it within the general mass of humanity. If each one of us did what was possible to do for whoever was standing right in front of our eyes, instead of goggling at the community of mankind, then all people, in aggregate, would at each moment be doing that which is needed by those in need, and by satisfying their needs, would establish the welfare of all mankind, which is made up of haves and have-nots, the weak and the strong.[6]

1. List practical reasons why it would have made sense for the Samaritan to pass by the stripped and wounded man on the road.

2. What unique justifications might the priest and Levite have had for walking past the man in need?

3. Every day God places people directly in our paths, and He asks us to show our love for Him by actively loving them (Luke 10:27). But we're so busy. There are so

---

[6] St. Theophan the Recluse, *The Spiritual Life: And How to Be Attuned to It* (Platina, CA: St. Herman of Alaska Brotherhood, 1955), 87, 93.

many urgent things that constantly require our attention. Which people have been placed in your path that you are tempted to walk around or ignore?

4. Saint Teresa of Calcutta wisely observed, "Loneliness and the feeling of being unwanted is the most terrible poverty." Service to the *heart* of another person is a true sharing of the love of God, and pleases Him deeply. One of the most overlooked places where significant ministry can occur is in our families. Real healing happens in the context of authentic, real relationships. Is there a person in your family that you find especially difficult to serve and love? We often avoid the people that we don't understand. In the words of author and speaker Bob Goff, "If I'm only willing to love the people who are nice to me, the ones who see things the way I do, and avoid all the rest, it's like reading every other page of the Bible and thinking I know what it says."[7] What is a concrete action you can take to love and serve a difficult family member?

Quiet your heart and enjoy His presence. . . . Ask Him to take the blinders off your eyes so you see the needs around you.

> *We ought not to be weary of doing little things for the love of God, who regards not the greatness of the work, but the love with which it is performed. We should not wonder if, in the beginning, we often fail in our endeavors, but that at last we shall gain a habit, which will naturally produce its acts in us, without our care, and to our exceeding great delight.*[8] — *Brother Lawrence*

God understands the things that keep us from serving our neighbor, but He loves us too much to let us remain content with such an isolated life. He encourages us to not get overwhelmed by the

---

[7] Bob Goff, *Everybody Always* (Nashville, TN: Thomas Nelson, 2018), 5.
[8] Brother Lawrence, *The Practice of the Presence of God* (New York: Image Books, 1977), 29.

mountain of need in the world, and to grow in our sensitivity to His gentle nudges as He prods us to reach out to those He places in our path each day.

Spend a few minutes asking God to help you to see interruptions in your day as opportunities to serve. These divine appointments that feel so inconvenient in the moment could be making an enormous difference in another's heart. We may never see just how significant these little acts of kindness are, but God sees. He knows. And nothing delights Him more than when we are sensitive enough to hear His whisper to pause and to love.

Day Three
TRYING TO "GO IT ALONE"

Read John 15:1–17.

1. In the parable of the vine and branches, who is represented by the vine, vine grower, and branches? According to John 15:4, what should be the branches' primary objective? What personal application can you draw from this verse?

2. John 15:10 reminds us that to remain in Christ's love, we need to keep His commandments. Summarize in your own words the commandment Jesus gave in John 15:12–17.

3. Author Mary Poplin wrote *Finding Calcutta* after spending a period of time serving alongside Saint Teresa of Calcutta. She had this to say about this saintly woman's perspective on her calling and service:

> Saint Teresa of Calcutta often referred to herself as a "pencil in God's hand." She believed that everything she was able to do was done by God's power working through her. Many people perceive Saint Teresa of Calcutta as someone who looked out at the poor and responded to their suffering with her own kindness, love and energy. This is not at all how Mother saw

her calling. When anyone complimented Saint Teresa of Calcutta, she would always say, "It is him, his work." She meant this literally—God did the work through her.[9]

Based upon what you have read in John 15, what part do you think Saint Teresa of Calcutta's humility played in the great work God did through her?

4. Have you experienced burnout or weariness because you were trying to serve sacrificially in your own strength? What encouragement do you gain from Philippians 4:13? What habits can you incorporate into your daily life so that the sap of the Holy Spirit runs from Christ the vine into you, the branch?

Quiet your heart and enjoy His presence. . . . Don't try to do it all alone. Christ waits each morning to infuse you with all you need.

Trying to bear fruit in our own strength is a recipe for disaster. We may start out with fervor, but at some point, God's call to love sacrificially will take us to a place beyond our own resources. Weariness and burnout will result. We'll want to quit.

The call we receive from Christ will always go beyond what we can do in our own strength. God has designed it this way to ensure that we don't turn our service for Him into a source of personal pride that draws our hearts far from Him.

God wants our service for Him to be what overflows from a heart filled with His grace. He pours in; we pour out. If we leave Him out of the picture, we'll settle for less than what we were created to do. We'll miss out on the abundant life He planned for each one of us personally.

There are specific works that God is calling each of His daughters to step out and do. We are His hands and feet in a broken world. But He insists that we not do this alone. Take a few moments to

---

[9] Mary Poplin, *Finding Calcutta: What Mother Teresa Taught Me About Meaningful Work and Service* (Downers Grove, IL: InterVarsity Press, 2008), 31.

place your open hands in His. Ask Him to infuse you with all you need to answer His call to serve. Trust that as you pray and ask Him to fill you, He will come with power and strength. Come, Lord Jesus, come!

Day Four
FEELING OVERWHELMED AT THE SIZE OF THE MOUNTAIN

Our reading for today takes place during a time when the Israelites were disobedient to God. In order to draw their hearts and focus back to Him, God allowed the Israelites to be attacked by Midianites (a group of camel nomads). The Israelites lived in constant fear and at real risk of starvation, because the Midianites would attack at harvest time and completely ransack the harvest, leaving nothing behind. The attacks caused them to cry out to God, asking Him to rescue them.

1. A. When the Israelites called out to God for rescue, He sent a messenger to a man named Gideon, telling him that he had been chosen as God's instrument to defeat the Midianites. Gideon gave the same sort of response that most of us do when God asks us to step out of our comfort zones. "Please, my Lord," he said, "how can *I* save Israel? My family is the poorest in Manasseh, and I am the most insignificant in my father's house." (Judges 6:15) What was God's response to Gideon's feelings of inadequacy? See Judges 6:15–16.

   God's response wasn't to say, "Come on, Gideon. You're so amazing! You just need to take a better look at all your amazing talents and gifts. You rock! You can do anything you set your mind to!" Instead, God simply said, "I will be with you." God's presence, the game changer. God's answer, the sure solution.

   B. When God asks you to step out of your comfort zone to serve Him, how do you usually respond? What words do you typically speak back to Him? How does His response to Gideon speak to you as you face your own inadequacies? Is He enough? Is His presence a game changer for you?

2. Back to Gideon . . . Once Gideon had established that God was truly calling him to step out to fight the Midianites, he gathered an army. Read about these

preparations in Judges 7:1–3 and comment on God's unusual take on the situation in verse 2.

3. Read Judges 7:4–8. The Israelites had gone from thirty-two thousand soldiers to ten thousand, but God continued to strip Gideon of resources. Describe how God cut down Gideon's manpower further and how many men remained after this.

4. Read Judges 7:9–22. What did God promise Gideon in verse 9? How did He strengthen Gideon's faith in verses 10–14? What weapons did the Israelite soldiers use in battle (verses 16–20)? Who actually killed the Midianites, according to verse 22?

Quiet your heart and enjoy His presence. . . . The battle belongs to the Lord.

Gideon faced impossible odds. He couldn't think of a person less likely to lead his people to deliverance than himself. And God kept stripping things down even further so that to the human eye, victory looked utterly unattainable. And think of the weapons the remaining three hundred soldiers were given! A trumpet, a jar, and a torch. As the jars were smashed to the ground, it symbolized each soldier's brokenness before God. But out of that brokenness, God brought victory.

Precious daughter of God, your very brokenness, your limitations, your inadequacies will be redeemed by God if only you will let Him. This is what He does. He takes the little we have to offer and infuses it with His limitless power. He frees us from our own places of bondage, and then gives us the strength and power to rescue others. So don't sit looking at your brokenness as the end of the story! It's only the beginning! Don't look at the size of the mountain before you! All the resources needed to scale it belong to your heavenly Father, and He will shower them upon you and share them with you because He is crazy about you. Don't hold back. Arise, for the Lord has delivered victory into your hands.

Day Five
PEOPLE CAN DRIVE YOU CRAZY

Let's get real. Sometimes the biggest thing that keeps us from persevering in serving is the people we're working alongside. They may look fine from a distance, but when you get up close and work hard together, day after day, all sorts of quirks and annoyances and bits of rudeness and prickles start coming out. We may be able to deal with it for a while, but once things begin to really hurt our feelings, we want to get out. Whatever passion we might have felt for this area of service can be quickly overshadowed by a pervading sense that *this is not fun anymore.*

1. Have you ever gotten so frustrated with someone you were serving alongside that you wanted to throw in the towel and go do something else? Think about that area of service. Was it something you were truly passionate about? Did you lean in toward the person in question, seeking to understand things from his or her perspective? Did you stuff your feelings and just ignore the problem? Did you get so tired of it or hurt that you walked away? Describe your response. Do you have any regrets?

2. Describe the hurts that Jesus experienced from those He was serving alongside. Remember that the people in these stories were His closest friends. See Mark 10:35–37, John 14:8–9, and Luke 22:47–48.

3. What allowed Jesus to persevere in His mission despite these intense hurts and disappointments? In other words, what helped Jesus to keep walking toward and then endure the cross? See Hebrews 12:2.

Jesus was able to endure the cross because He focused on "the joy that was set before Him." What does that mean? What was the joy that He was focusing on? Was it just relief, knowing that His pain and suffering would be over soon? No. His joy was rooted in the knowledge that His suffering had a purpose. It was going to purchase our redemption. It was going to free all of us from the grip of sin. He was *over* seeing people enslaved by and entangled in sin. He knew that what He was suffering would be worth it when He could see us walking in freedom and closeness to God.

4. Jesus persevered through the frustration of working with people who just didn't get it, who made insensitive comments, who betrayed Him, who spit on Him, who beat Him, and who crucified Him because He never lost sight of the fact that it all had a purpose. That purpose was costly, but it was worth it. What about you? Read Hebrews 12:1–4. What joy could you set before your eyes that might help you persevere in serving, despite the frustrations you're feeling? What perspective do you gain from Hebrews 12:4?

Quiet your heart and enjoy His presence. . . . Pray for those who persecute you.

Are you currently experiencing frustration with someone you are serving alongside? Instead of thinking about what's bothering you, spend some time praying for this person. Ask God to help you to see things from the other person's perspective. Commit to Him that you will determine where and how you serve—not based on how you are feeling or how much fun it is at the present time, but instead based on what God is asking you to do. Ask Him to make His will clear and to give you His eyes so that you look on everyone, especially the person who is frustrating you, through a filter of compassion.

Conclusion

Joining Christ in the deeper work of bringing the gospel to the darkest places—the hurt within that so few can access—requires suffering. And that flies in the face of our deep-seated hope of avoiding anything painful or difficult in life. Make no mistake, if we serve Christ with this underlying desire (freedom from suffering), we'll be greatly hindered in our effectiveness. Jesus needs servants who don't count the cost, who are willing to go to the depths for His sake. Who are willing to get back up again when they are weary. Who are able to recognize that it takes "a lot of humiliations to produce a little bit of humility,"[10] and humility is required if Jesus is going to do the work through us; we're just going to be His pencils.

But isn't He worth it? Isn't He worth everything? What did He hold back from us? When He counted the cost, He looked at us and said, "I'm in this for the long haul. I love each one of these women so much that there is nothing that I won't endure for them." But the thing is, He doesn't just love the churchgoers, the people who do good deeds, and the ladies who devote their lives to ministry. He loves everyone. He loves the awkward person in your life who wants a friendship when you want space. He loves the homeless man who smells funny. He loves the orphan in Africa. He loves the kid at the mall who is walking around with his pants halfway down his legs and his boxers sticking out. He loves all of us equally. And He sees into all our hearts, and knows that we all need a hand. We need tenderness. We need mercy.

So He asks us, "Will you be my hands? Will you show my heart? Will you act toward people (the ones you really want to turn away from) the way that I would act toward them? Because that's the only way they're going to see me."

My Resolution

"My Resolution" is your opportunity to write down one specific, personal application from this lesson. We can take in a lot of information from studying the Bible, but if we don't translate it into action, we have totally missed the point. In James 1:22, we're told that we shouldn't just hear the word of God, we are to "do what it says." So what qualities should be found in a good resolution? It should be **personal** (use the pronouns I, me, my, mine), it should be **possible** (don't choose something so far fetched that you'll just become discouraged), it should be **measurable** (a specific goal

---

[10] Poplin, 106.

to achieve within a specific time period) and it should be **action-oriented** (not just a spiritual thought.)

Examples:

1. I'll set aside a time this week to turn off my phone and other electronics, and really think about what problem in the world bothers me enough that I am asking, "Who is going to do something about this?!" Then I'll ask God if He is calling me.

2. As I look at areas where I'm serving, I'll check to see if I'm trying to do things in my own strength, or if I'm relying on God and asking him to do the work *through* me. I'll test this by comparing how much I pray about this area of service and how much time I simply spend working.

3. There is someone I am serving alongside who is driving me crazy. I'm considering quitting to get a little relief. Instead of doing this, I'm going to lean in. I'm going to set up a time to get face-to-face with this person and seek to understand things from his or her perspective.

My Resolution:

Catechism Clips

CCC 1936 On coming into the world, man is not equipped with everything he needs for developing his bodily and spiritual life. He needs others. Differences appear tied to age, physical abilities, intellectual or moral aptitudes, the benefits derived from social commerce, and the distribution of wealth. The "talents" are not distributed equally.

CCC 1937 These differences belong to God's plan, who wills that each receive what he needs from others, and that those endowed with particular "talents" share the benefits with those who need them. These differences encourage and often oblige persons to practice generosity, kindness, and sharing of goods; they foster the mutual enrichment of cultures:

I distribute the virtues quite diversely; I do not give all of them to each person, but some to one, some to others. . . . I shall give principally charity to one; justice to another; humility to this one, a living faith to that one. . . . And so I have given many gifts and graces, both spiritual and temporal, with such diversity that I have not given everything to one single person, so that you may be constrained to practice charity towards one another. . . . I have willed that one should need another and that all should be my ministers in distributing the graces and gifts they have received from me.

Verse Study

See Appendix 2 for instructions on how to complete a verse study.

Matthew 20:26–27

1. Verse:

2. Paraphrase:

3. Questions:

4. Cross-references:

5. Personal Application:

Lesson 2

BALANCE THROUGH CONTENTMENT

Introduction

"For the first time, she did want more. She did not know what she wanted, knew that it was dangerous and that she should rest content with what she had, but she knew an emptiness deep inside her, which began to ache." —Iain Pears, *The Dream of Scipio*

Sometimes lack of contentment is ill-defined emotion. We're unsettled, longing for more, but unclear what would fill the void within. Other times we know exactly what would make us feel better. We can point to a specific circumstance that is causing our discontent.

We also experience seasons of life when our circumstances are more or less the way we want them to be. This can lead us to mistake those feelings of satisfaction for true contentment. But in the words of Dr. David Jeremiah, "If you are not content in challenging circumstances, the contentment you think you feel in other circumstances is not contentment but simply your satisfaction that things are momentarily the way you think they should be."[11]

Saint Paul leads the way in giving us a beautiful example of contentment. He wrote the following while imprisoned, which gives his words added weight:

Not that I say this because of need, for I have learned, in whatever situation I find myself, to be self-sufficient. I know indeed how to live in humble circumstances; I know also how to live with abundance. In every circumstance and in all things I have learned the secret of being well fed and of going hungry, of living in abundance and of being in need. I have the strength for everything through him who empowers me. (Philippians 4:11–13)

---

[11] David Jeremiah, "Turning Point with Dr. David Jeremiah: Contentment—When Enough Is Enough," Oneplace.com, www.oneplace.com/ministries/turning-point/read/articles/contentment--when-enough-is-enough-13954.html.

Note that Saint Paul did not say, "I was born with an extraordinary ability to be content in the midst of suffering." He said, "I have learned." This should greatly encourage us. Contentment can be learned. It doesn't depend on our circumstances. No matter where we are, regardless of our track record, we can grow in the area of contentment.

There are many things that get in the way of this pursuit. Throughout this lesson, we'll look at five barriers to contentment, and the ways we can break through them and experience the freedom that comes from being satisfied with what God has already provided.

Day One
BARRIER #1: AN OVERWHELMING DESIRE FOR MORE

1. According to Ecclesiastes 2:10–11 and CCC 2536, how much is enough? Will more possessions or money satisfy us?

"Give a man everything he wants and in that moment everything will not be everything." —Immanuel Kant

2. Where does our material wealth come from? Who is the true owner of all we possess? See 1 Chronicles 29:11–12.

3. Read the following excerpt from Os Guinness' book *The Call*, paying attention to the difficulty we have in differentiating needs from wants:

   From the Greeks and Romans down to many modern people, a simple piety has reigned: the notion that we can solve the problem of money by distinguishing between "needs" and "surplus," between "necessities" and "luxuries." Carnegie, for example, held that philanthropy was the business of "administering surplus wealth." But what if we can never settle on the balance? What if one person's luxuries are another's necessities? Can't we always rationalize how much is enough?[12]

A. Take a few moments to meditate on your spending. If you were willing to choose a simpler or less expensive option over a more luxurious one, then give away the money saved, what could that provide for someone in need? Does meditating on that thought impact your level of contentment?

This excerpt continues:

> The problem is that money can assume an inordinate place in our lives until it becomes a personal, spiritual, god-like force that rules us—Mammon. Jesus' use of *Mammon* (Aramaic for *wealth*) is unique—he gave it a strength and precision that the word never had before. He did not usually personify things, let alone deify them. And neither the Jews nor the nearby pagans knew a god by this name. But what Jesus says in speaking of Mammon is that money is a power—and not in a vague sense, as in the "force" of words. Rather, money is a power in the sense that it is an active agent with decisive spiritual power and is never neutral. It is a power before we use it, not simply as we use it or whether we use it well or badly. As such, Mammon is a genuine rival to God. . . . Either we serve God and use money or we serve money and use God.[13]

B. Do you agree with these statements? Why or why not?

---

[12] Os Guinness, *The Call: Finding and Fulfilling the Central Purpose of Your Life* (Nashville, TN: W Publishing Group, 1998), 133.
[13] Ibid., 133–134.

4. In Matthew 6:19–21, Jesus said, "Do not store up for yourselves treasures on earth, where moth and decay destroy, and thieves break in and steal. But store up treasures in heaven, where neither moth nor decay destroys, nor thieves break in and steal. For where your treasure is, there also will your heart be." What are some practical ways you can treasure the things that matter most instead of feeding your appetite for more possessions?

Quiet your heart and enjoy His presence. . . . You alone will satisfy the longings of my heart.

To break down the barrier to contentment of an overwhelming desire for more, pray Psalm 63.

O God, you are my God—
it is you I seek!
For you my body yearns;
for you my soul thirsts,
In a land parched, lifeless,
and without water.
I look to you in the sanctuary
to see your power and glory.
For your love is better than life;
my lips shall ever praise you!

I will bless you as long as I live;
I will lift up my hands, calling on your name.
My soul shall be sated as with choice food,
with joyous lips my mouth shall praise you!
I think of you upon my bed,
I remember you through the watches of the night
You indeed are my savior,
and in the shadow of your wings I shout for joy.
My soul clings fast to you;
your right hand upholds me. (Psalm 63:1–8)

Day Two
BARRIER #2: LACK OF PURPOSE

Lack of purpose is a barrier to contentment. When we don't know why we are here on earth, we often seek fulfillment and purpose in the wrong places. Sometimes we experience discontent because we don't seem to be doing anything that really matters. This can discourage us, causing us to settle for mediocrity instead of the great purpose God created us for. Other times we experience discontent because we *have* measured up and achieved our goals, but they were the wrong goals. We now realize that having achieved them doesn't satisfy us the way we expected. Contentment is intricately tied to recognizing the *true* purpose of our existence and spending our time accordingly. To discover it, we must start with the one who created us.

1. CCC 27 is a great starting point for understanding why we are here. Read it and answer the following questions.

   What is written in the human heart, and why?

   What does God never cease to do?

   Where is the only place that we will find the truth and happiness that we never stop searching for?

   What does our dignity rest on?

If a woman exists, it's because God created her through love, and through love continues to sustain her existence. What does a woman need to do to live fully according to that truth?

2. Read Paul Bradshaw's interview with Rick Warren, found in Appendix 4. What insights do you gain from his perspective on the purpose of life? In what way do his words confirm the truth found in CCC 27?

What is the purpose of your life? It's bigger than personal fulfillment, feeling an inner peace, or being happy. It's bigger than marrying the right person or pursuing a certain career. **Your purpose here on earth is to know God and become more like Him.** Every longing, disappointment, and circumstance needs to be filtered through that truth.

3. Life is meant to be an adventure. Even though we'll experience suffering and disappointment, those circumstances give us the opportunity to fulfill our life purpose. Each day, God calls out to us through the events He allows to intersect our lives. We need to be ready to listen to Him in the midst of the circumstances, asking how He is calling us to respond. What does 2 Timothy 1:9 say regarding God's call to each of us?

4. Think of an area of your life where you are experiencing discontent. Look at that circumstance through the lens of your true purpose. How is God calling you to respond? In what way can you know God better and become more like Him in the midst of your current difficulty?

Quiet your heart and enjoy His presence. . . . You will find Him here.

Contentment comes when we know we're living right in the middle of God's will. When we are able to look at all our circumstances as a means to fulfill our true purpose—knowing God and becoming more like Him—we are able to go through life thankfully. Expressing thanks is a key to contentment. Our circumstances don't change, but our perspective does. This change in perspective equips us to "offer [our] bodies as a living sacrifice, holy and pleasing to God, [which is our] spiritual worship." (Romans 12:1)

Spend a few minutes in prayer, offering yourself to God. If you feel ready, offer Him your area of discontent. Ask Him to achieve His purpose in you through this difficulty. If you aren't at a point where you feel able to do that, you could ask Him to help you to want to know Him and become like Him more than you desire anything else.

Day Three
BARRIER #3: ANXIETY

Note: There is anxiety common to all, feelings of worry, unease and nervousness. And then there is a far deeper anxiety, one that results in panic attacks, is connected to post-traumatic stress disorder, obsessions and compulsions. This lesson does not attempt to address these more significant levels of anxiety. If that is where you find yourself today, please know that you are not alone, there is help and there is hope. If anxiety is significantly impacting your quality of life, I encourage you to seek professional help because true change and healing is possible.

Anxiety is a barrier to contentment. It grips our emotions, harms our health, and leads our thoughts down a path that culminates with fear. Often we feel we can't get out from under our anxious thoughts, which take on a life of their own as we imagine worst-case scenarios. These thoughts often omit God from the picture. We see ourselves as alone and unable to cope. In the words of Linda Dillow, "Anxiety is that which divides and distracts the soul, that which diverts us from present duty to weary calculations of how to meet conditions that may never arrive. It's the habit of crossing bridges before we reach them."[14]

Archbishop Fulton Sheen put it strongly when he said, "All worry is atheism, because it is a want of trust in God." Let's grow in our trust of God, and begin to break down this barrier to contentment.

1. Read 1 Peter 5:6–7 and answer the questions below.

   What does this verse instruct us to do with our anxieties?

   Why can we confidently do this?

   What are we told to do before we cast our worries upon God?

When we are humble, we acknowledge that God is God, and we are not. True humility involves surrender and a total trust in God alone. It comes when we recognize that only God can take care of the things that are making us anxious. Our cares and concerns are safe in His hands.

2. What are you anxious about? List your worries here. When these worries fill your mind, are you thinking about God's presence in the midst of them? When they involve your loved ones, do you picture Him by their side?

---

[14] Linda Dillow, *Calm My Anxious Heart: A Woman's Guide to Finding Contentment* (Colorado Springs: NavPress, 1998), 120.

The oriental shepherd always walked *ahead* of his sheep. He was always *out in front*. Any attack upon the sheep had to take him into account first. Now God is out in front. He is in our tomorrows, and it is tomorrow that fills people with fear. *Yet God is already there.* All the tomorrows of our life have to pass through Him before they can get to us.[15] —F. B. Meyer

"Worry does not empty tomorrow of its sorrow; it empties today of its strength." — Corrie ten Boom

3. When we are anxious, a battle rages in our minds and hearts. Even when we want to trust God, thoughts spring up, and before we know it, we are going down the path of worry. God does not leave us alone to fight this mental battle. Describe the weapons He provides for us according to 2 Corinthians 10:4–5 and Ephesians 6:13–18.

   2 Corinthians 10:4–5

   Ephesians 6:13–18

4. When an anxious thought comes into your mind, you have a choice regarding how you will respond. Will you play with it? Will you travel with it into the future in your imagination? Or will you stop it in its tracks, grab hold of the thought, and offer it to Christ? This is what is meant by 2 Corinthians 10:5: "Take every thought captive in obedience to Christ." Take it captive by replacing the worry with a truth that builds your trust in God. Look back on today's verses and quotes. Record one below that helps you regain perspective in the face of anxiety. Write it

---

[15] L. B. Cowman, *Streams in the Desert*, ed. James Reimann (Grand Rapids, MI: Zondervan, 1997), 32.

on an index card to carry with you so that when anxiety hits, you can replace that thought with God's truth.

Note: For deeper study on how to take every thought captive to Christ, we recommend the Walking with Purpose Bible study, *Fearless and Free: Finding Healing and Wholeness in Christ.*

Quiet your heart and enjoy His presence. . . . He is in your tomorrows.

Read the following words from the devotional Jesus Calling, *as if they were Jesus' words to you:*

Anxiety is the result of envisioning the future without Me. So the best defense against worry is staying in communication with Me. When you turn your thoughts toward Me, you can think much more positively. Remember to listen, as well as to speak, making your thoughts a dialogue with Me.

If you must consider upcoming events, follow these rules: 1) Do not linger in the future, because anxieties sprout like mushrooms when you wander there. 2) Remember the promise of My continual Presence, include Me in any imagery that comes to mind. This mental discipline does not come easily, because you are accustomed to being a god of your fantasies. However, the reality of My Presence with you, now and forevermore, outshines any fantasy you could ever imagine.[16]

Perhaps you are a planner, and part of the way that you process what might come is by picturing the worst-case scenario and coming up with a game plan. It might feel impossible to discipline your mind not to peer into the future. If that's the case, make sure that you picture God in the midst of those imagined future circumstances instead of picturing yourself trying to cope alone.

---

[16] Sarah Young, *Jesus Calling: Enjoying Peace in His Presence* (Nashville, TN: Thomas Nelson, 2004), 304.

Day Four
BARRIER #4: FEELING STUCK

Another barrier to contentment is feeling stuck in our current circumstances. We feel constraints that we perceive to be crowding out any chance at joy. The discontent may be rooted in an unsatisfying relationship, financial hardship, physical disability, illness, or intense unfulfilled longings. We can feel stuck because of grief, or stuck with bad habits that we can't seem to get rid of. These stuck places are exactly where God wants to meet us. He ushers in hope. He decimates barriers. By His grace, let's break free!

1. The book of Exodus describes the Israelites' four hundred years of slavery in Egypt. They were mistreated terribly and cried out to God. God sent them a rescuer, Moses, who led them out of Egypt and toward true freedom. The memories of God's mind-blowing miracles should have stayed fresh in their minds, but travel to the Promised Land proved to be a little tougher than they'd expected. How did they respond to their experience of feeling stuck? See Exodus 16:2–3.

2. God met the Israelites in their place of need and provided manna for them to eat as they wandered in the wilderness. The problem was, that was *all* He provided. And they got sick of manna. Manna for breakfast, lunch, and dinner got pretty old. They began thinking Egypt hadn't been so bad ("sure we were slaves, but the variety of food was pretty great") and started to complain again. They wanted meat, so God said He'd send them meat. What did He say about how much meat would be sent, and why was He sending it like this? See Numbers 11:18–20.

In essence, the Israelites shook their fists at God and said, "We were better off when we didn't know you!" We might be shocked by how quickly they failed to remember God's goodness, but aren't we often guilty of the same forgetfulness?

When God leaves us in the stuck places, we can wrongly conclude that nothing good can happen there. We look back, or fantasize about a different life, and we see fertile ground where great things could grow. Then we look at our current place and see barrenness, loss, heaviness. When we're in these stuck places, we have to guard our hearts, because there is something about those circumstances that can lead us to conclude that we would be better off without God. And nothing could be further from the truth.

The truth is, when we are stuck, we are deep in fertile ground. This is rich soil for transformation and growth. It's in this place that we can see God's provision and care for us in a whole new way. He may not provide an emergency exit from our problems; He may instead give us the grace to keep walking through them, day by day, hour by hour, minute by minute. Regardless of how He provides, He will be faithful. And we will see Him in a whole new light, and be forever changed because of it. If we cooperate. If we trust.

3. What does Philippians 4:19 say that God promises to provide?

4. It's important to note that Philippians 4:19 does not say that God promises to supply all of our *wants*, only our *needs*. Reflect back on your life purpose. Do you see evidence of the way that God is supplying all you need to fulfill your purpose? Do your wants ever get in the way of that pursuit? Do you find it hard to differentiate between your needs and your wants?

Quiet your heart and enjoy His presence. . . . In your presence there is fullness of joy.

Contentment comes when our focus shifts from our limitations and instead we recognize all the riches that we are given through Christ. Meditate on Psalm 103:1–5, and thank God for the gifts that cost Him everything to give.

> *Bless the Lord, my soul;*
> *All my being, bless his holy name!*
> *Bless the Lord, my soul;*
> *And do not forget all his gifts,*
> *Who pardons all your sins,*

And heals all your ills,
Who redeems your life from the pit,
And crowns you with mercy and compassion,
Who fills your days with good things,
So your youth is renewed like the eagle's.

Day Five
BARRIER #5: SETTLING FOR MUD PIES

A final barrier to contentment is our tendency to turn away from Christ and all the fullness He offers and instead settle for cheap substitutes. We may believe that we are pursuing and achieving what matters most, but then we experience discontent when the pleasures those things bring don't satisfy as we expected. In the words of C. S. Lewis:

> If we consider the unblushing promises of reward and the staggering nature of the rewards promised in the Gospels, it would seem that our Lord finds our desires not too strong, but too weak. We are half-hearted creatures, fooling about with drink and sex and ambition when infinite joy is offered us, like an ignorant child who wants to go on making mudpies in a slum because he cannot imagine what is meant by an offer of a holiday at the sea. We are far too easily pleased.[17]

We don't know what we're missing. Let's spend our final day of study taking a look at the riches of Christ, in hopes that we'll desire Him above all else and find contentment that is not dependent on our circumstances.

1. Read Colossians 1:15–20, and record any words or phrases that describe the all-sufficiency and greatness of Christ.

He is more than enough.

---

[17] C. S. Lewis, "The Weight of Glory," in *The Weight of Glory and Other Addresses*, ed. W. Hooper (New York: Simon & Shuster, 1996), 25–26.

2. In Colossians 1:17, we read that in Jesus "all things hold together." This is true for creation—He owns and sustains the order and breath of all on the earth. But it is also true in our lives. Any area of our lives that is not connected to Christ is at great risk of falling apart. Is there something falling apart in your life? Have you come to the end of your resources? How can you invite Christ to hold it together for you?

3. 1 Peter 1:4 describes your heavenly inheritance. Write this verse in your own words.

4. Contrary to what we may believe, we do not *need* to be free from financial constraints, emotional heartache, physical illness, and all suffering. What we *need* is Christ. Read 1 Peter 1:6–7. What benefit can come from our trials if we cooperate?

All the things that can lead us to discontent are actually opportunities to experience freedom. We aren't promised that we'll be free of suffering and pain, but right in the middle of those difficult circumstances, God is offering us the opportunity to be freed from the desire for human approval, the attitude of entitlement that says, "I deserve," the urge to be right, the longing to be in control, the grip of fear, the pit of self-pity. We don't have to wait until heaven to experience true freedom. It's on offer to us today.

Quiet your heart and enjoy His presence. . . . Start enjoying your inheritance in Christ today.

In the letter to the Ephesians, Saint Paul pleaded with the Church to recognize their glorious inheritance. Meditate on the following passages, letting your heart be filled with awareness of all you've been given by the One who loves you with abandon.

"In him we were also chosen, destined in accord with the purpose of the One who accomplishes all things according to the intention of his will." (Ephesians 1:11)

Meditate on what it means to be chosen by God.

Paul prayed "that the God of our Lord Jesus Christ, the Father of glory, may give you a spirit of wisdom and revelation resulting in your knowledge of him." (Ephesians 1:17)

Meditate on what it means to be given a spirit of wisdom and revelation that helps us know Christ more intimately.

"May the eyes of your hearts be enlightened, that you may know what is the hope that belongs to his call, what are the riches of glory in his inheritance among the holy ones." (Ephesians 1:18)

Meditate on all the hope that's included in a call from God—a call to learn from every difficult circumstance, a call to grow and be transformed in the fertile soil of suffering.

Meditate on how glorious it will be to experience our inheritance in heaven. Imagine standing before the throne of Christ. Drink in His majesty. Soak up His mercy and goodness.

Never forget that a part of your inheritance experienced on earth is "the surpassing greatness of his power for us who believe, in accord with the exercise of his great might, which he worked in Christ, raising him from the dead and setting him at his right hand in the heavens, far above every principality, authority, power, and dominion, and every name that is named not only in this age but also in the one to come." (Ephesians 1:19–21)

Meditate on the resurrection power that was strong enough to raise Jesus from the dead. That's the power He offers you every day. Why would we ever settle for less?

Conclusion

"God has no other reason for creating than his love and goodness: 'Creatures came into existence when the key of love opened his hand.'" (CCC 293)

You are so dearly loved. It was God's personal love for you that caused Him to call you into existence. You are here on earth to experience a journey that originates in His hand (opened with the key of love), reflects that love throughout a lifetime, and then returns to His embrace in heaven.

Our purpose on earth is to prepare for the place where we'll experience the deepest contentment. "For here we have no lasting city, but we seek the one that is to come." (Hebrews 13:14) Through the riches of Christ Jesus, we have been given everything we need to make that journey.

And what a vision is waiting for us there! What fullness we'll experience when we come face-to-face with our Rescuer. There we'll find "the Lamb who is in the center of the throne, [and He] will shepherd [us] and lead [us] to springs of life-giving water, and God will wipe away every tear from [our] eyes." (Revelation 7:17)

What are our Rescuer's words for us today, when we are in the midst of this journey? Personalize these words from the book of Revelation: "I know your works (behold, I have left an open door before you, which no one can close). You have limited strength, and yet you have kept my word and have not denied my name. . . . Because you have kept my message of endurance, I will keep you safe in the time of trial. . . . I am coming quickly. Hold fast to what you have, so that no one may take your crown." (Revelation 3:8–11)

Hold fast to the All-Sufficient One. Let His fullness be yours. True contentment is found in Him.

My Resolution

In what specific way will I apply what I learned in this lesson?

Examples:

1. I will make a list of my current wants, and ask the Lord if what I consider a necessity is actually a luxury when seen from the perspective of someone in need. Is God asking me to let go of something I'd like to have, so that I can be more generous with those less financially fortunate than I am?

2. When an anxious thought springs into my mind, I will take that thought captive to Christ, and imagine the potential future event with Him by my side.

3. Before I present my requests to God in prayer, I will meditate on Colossians 1:15–20. This will help me to recognize the greatness of Christ, and will remind me that He is more than enough for me.

My Resolution:

Catechism Clips

CCC 27 The desire for God is written in the human heart, because man is created by God and for God; and God never ceases to draw man to himself. Only in God will he find the truth and happiness he never stops searching for:

> The dignity of man rests above all on the fact that he is called to communion with God. This invitation to converse with God is addressed to man as soon as he comes into being. For if man exists it is because God has created him through love, and through love continues to hold him in existence. He cannot live fully according to truth unless he freely acknowledges that love and entrusts himself to his creator.

CCC 293 Scripture and Tradition never cease to teach and celebrate this fundamental truth: "The world was made for the glory of God." St. Bonaventure explains that God created all things "not to increase his glory, but to show it forth and to communicate it", for God has no other reason for creating than his love and goodness: "Creatures came into existence when the key of love opened his hand." The First Vatican Council explains:

> This one, true God, of his own goodness and "almighty power", not for increasing his own beatitude, nor for attaining his perfection, but in order to manifest this perfection through the benefits which he bestows on creatures, with absolute freedom of counsel "and from the beginning of time, made out of nothing both orders of creatures, the spiritual and the corporeal. . ."

CCC 2536 The tenth commandment forbids greed and the desire to amass earthly goods without limit. It forbids avarice arising from a passion for riches and their attendant power. It also forbids the desire to commit injustice by harming our neighbor in his temporal goods:

When the Law says, "You shall not covet," these words mean that we should banish our desires for whatever does not belong to us. Our thirst for another's goods is immense, infinite, never quenched. Thus it is written: "He who loves money never has money enough."

Verse Study

See Appendix 2 for instructions on how to complete a verse study.

1 Timothy 6:6-8

1. Verse:

2. Paraphrase:

3. Questions:

4. Cross-references:

   •

4. Personal Application:

NOTES

Lesson 3

BALANCING OUR CRAVINGS

Introduction

You know a friend really loves you when she can reel off your favorite snacks from memory without an ounce of judgment. I have such a friend, and she knows my affinity for Johnson's caramel corn, from Ocean City, N.J., and pretzel M&M's. In fact, when she comes to visit, she often leaves these treats behind in surprise locations. So I'll sit down at my desk and my feet will kick a tub of caramel corn, or I'll open a kitchen drawer and be greeted by pretzel M&M's. I, of course, immediately feel called to eat these treats, because ignoring them would be bad manners. I figure it's like not opening a present when someone clearly wants you to. So I have to tell you, when I sat down to write this lesson on balancing our cravings, I started really craving pretzel M&M's. I convinced myself that there was no point writing until my craving was satisfied, and so I began my search. It was like *Where's Waldo?* in real life. I can now settle down in front of the computer, because I found them in my filing cabinet. She wins the best friend award for the day.

We eat for all sorts of reasons. Sometimes it's for comfort, or because we're sad. Other times we eat because we're lonely. Food can be our reward or how we celebrate an important event. Interestingly, none of those reasons have anything to do with physical hunger.

Here in the land of plenty, we have turned food into something that God never intended it to be, and it's killing us both physically and spiritually. Does that sound extreme? It depends on how you see the world. Matthew Kelly gives us an interesting picture of the world:

> Today there are seven billion people on the planet, but imagine for a moment that the whole world is a village of one hundred people. If we reduced the world's population to one hundred people, proportionally, this is how the world would look: Fifty-seven of those one hundred people would come from Asia, twenty-one from Europe, nine from Africa, eight from North America,

and five from South America. Fifty-one would be women and forty-nine would be men. Six of those one hundred people would own or control more than 50 percent of the world's wealth, and five of these six people would be U.S. citizens. One of those one hundred people would have just been born, one would be just about to die, and only one of those one hundred people would have been to college. Thirty-three would be Christian and sixty-seven would be non-Christian. Eighty would be living in substandard housing. Thirty-one would be unable to read and write. Twenty-four would have no electricity. Seventy-one would not have access to the Internet. Thirty-nine of the one hundred people in the village would live on less than two dollars a day. One-third of the world's population is dying from lack of bread, one-third of the world's population is dying from lack of justice, and one-third of the world's population is dying from overeating. How do you see the world?[18]

As we turn to food for reasons other than genuine hunger, we create or strengthen a blind spot toward people who are genuinely hungry and need our help. Our focus turns inward, and we choose instant gratification over selfless living so that others can live.

As I write this, I am preaching to myself. I struggle with this. But I want to change. I'm tired of feeling ruled by my cravings. Is there a better way? Are we stuck, or can we, with God's help, come to a place of freedom in regard to food? Could that freedom lead to actions that can be life changing for us and for those in need? Absolutely. "For God, all things are possible." (Matthew 19:26) This week, we're going to explore this better way. May we grasp it with both hands and be transformed.

Day One
WHY IT MATTERS

1. Do you find yourself falling into patterns of turning to food for reasons other than physical hunger? What circumstances or emotions cause you to crave in this way?

---

[18] Matthew Kelly, *The Four Signs of a Dynamic Catholic: How Engaging 1% of Catholics Could Change the World* (Hebron, KY: Beacon Publishing, 2012), 75–76.

2. If you have tried to balance your cravings in the past, has the motive been weight loss, or have you had a sense that food has a hold on you and you want to be free?

3. What do Proverbs 31:30 and 1 Peter 3:3–4 tell us about beauty from God's perspective? Are we to balance our cravings because God wants us to fit into a smaller pant size?

4. Balancing our cravings is not about losing weight or getting closer to our culture's unattainable standard of outward beauty. It has everything to do with *why* we are craving to begin with. God created us to crave, or to feel restless, so that we'd long for more. Whether we realize it or not, what are our souls truly longing for? See Psalm 42:2–3, 63:2–3, and CCC 2557.

Quiet your heart and enjoy His presence. . . . You were made for more.

The cravings we feel won't be satiated with coffee, sweets, or salty treats. We were made to crave connection to the One who created us. Lysa TerKeurst says it well in her book Made to Crave:

We were made for more than this. More than this failure, more than this cycle, more than being ruled by taste buds. We were made for victory. Sometimes we just have to find our way to that truth. . . .

Food can fill our stomachs but never our souls.
Possessions can fill our houses but never our hearts.
Sex can fill our nights but never our hunger for love.

Children can fill our days but never our identities.
Jesus wants us to know only He can fill us and truly satisfy us.[19]

Do we know how desperately Jesus wants to fill up our empty places? He longs for us to taste the true satisfaction that comes from satiating our cravings with Him. When we are lonely, sad, or angry, or we need to celebrate, He wants us to turn to Him instead of to a cookie or chips. Jesus is "the one who fills all things in every way." (Ephesians 1:23)

Take some time to talk to Him about the way you are most likely to respond to emotional ups and downs. If you typically turn somewhere other than to Him, ask Him to work in your heart so that when the emotion hits, you remember to turn to Him first. Thank Him for being enough. Thank Him for being the only One who truly satisfies the cravings of our hearts. Why does it matter what we do with our cravings? It matters because we were made for more, and God wants that to be our experience.

Day Two
IRRESISTIBLE

1. Do you find yourself craving certain foods or drinks to the point that you would consider yourself enslaved by them? Are there certain foods or drinks that you feel you just can't live without? If so, what are they?

2. What insight does Saint Paul give us in 1 Corinthians 6:12 regarding being dominated or enslaved by our cravings?

Food is not sinful. But because we aren't to be ruled by anything other than God, being enslaved to food or drink is a form of idolatry. An idol is anything that we allow to take the place of God in our lives. Anything that controls us falls into this category.

---

[19] Lysa TerKeurst, *Made to Crave: Satisfying Your Deepest Desire with God, Not Food* (Grand Rapids, MI: Zondervan, 2010), 49, 64.

It benefits us to give control of our lives to God, because He loves us lavishly and wants what's best for us. The same cannot be said for food, which can have a hold on us to the point of being destructive.

God wants us to enjoy food as a beautiful gift from Him, but He doesn't want it to rule our hearts. Eating in secret, running to food instead of running to God, and feeling unable to say no to our cravings are indicators that certain foods, while lawful, are not beneficial to us.

3. When we realize that we are enslaved to certain foods, drinks, or habits, it's easy to get discouraged and feel powerless to change. What power is described in Ephesians 1:18–20? Is this power available to us? What hope does this passage give you in the struggle to grow in self-discipline?

4. Galatians 5:22–23 describes the fruits of the Spirit. Which fruit of the Spirit do you need in order to conquer your cravings?

Quiet your heart and enjoy His presence. . . . Connecting your heart to His will transform you from the inside out.

We have access to a power that is beyond us. We can live differently! All the fruits of the Holy Spirit can be displayed in our lives. But we don't get them by trying hard. The Holy Spirit produces them in us as we connect to Christ. Jesus described this process in John 15:5 when He said, "I am the vine; you are the branches. If a man remains in me and I in him, he will bear much fruit; apart from me you can do nothing." As we spend time with Him, His character traits are infused into us.

Ask Jesus to fill you with the fruit of the Spirit that you most need right now. Take the time to quietly sit in His presence, enjoying His unconditional love. Imagine His love pouring over you, filling any empty places and strengthening you where you are weak.

Day Three
JESUS' FAVORITE FOOD

Read John 4:31–35.

1. What food was Jesus talking about in John 4:34?

2. What did Jesus tell His disciples to look up and see in John 4:35?

Jesus wasn't suggesting that we aren't supposed to eat actual food. He was just raising awareness of the fact that when we are searching for satisfaction, nothing fulfills us like doing God's will. We were made for more. There's something bigger that God wants us to be a part of. It's bigger than temporarily satisfying our cravings with food. Getting our eyes off of ourselves and onto the needs of others alters our perspective and empowers us to change. There is a calling, a mission, with your name on it. When you discover what that is and begin living it out, you'll experience a rush that is far superior to anything food or drink temporarily offers.[20]

3. If we allow our minds to dwell on what we know we shouldn't have, our desire for it will only intensify. God wants us to satisfy our cravings with Him, and switch our focus from food to doing His will. Satan will continually try to keep us from doing that. This has always been his tactic. When Jesus was preparing for His public ministry by fasting in the desert, Satan tried to get Him to focus on how satisfying loaves of bread would be. What did Jesus say in response to Satan tempting Him to take His focus off of doing God's will? See Matthew 4:4.

[20] The Catherine of Siena Institute offers excellent resources to help you discern your charisms (spiritual gifts) and calling. These resources can be found on the institute's website, siena.org.

4. In his letter to the Philippians, Saint Paul wrote about people whose "God is their stomach . . . their minds are occupied with earthly things." (Philippians 3:19) We are told to "Think of what is above, not on what is on earth." (Colossians 3:2) When we are craving food for reasons other than genuine hunger, our focus is on earthly things. Just as Jesus was sustained by the Word of God in the desert, Scripture can sustain us in our times of temptation. The Holy Spirit can use Bible verses to bring our focus back to living in a self-controlled way that pleases God. Write out the following verses, and choose the one that you find most helpful in combating cravings. Write it out on an index card, and read it to yourself when you are tempted to eat something that, while lawful, wouldn't be beneficial to you.

Romans 8:37

1 Corinthians 10:13

1 Corinthians 10:23

Quiet your heart and enjoy His presence. . . . Nothing satisfies like doing God's will.

As much as we think the sugar rush or salty fix will satisfy us, nothing tastes as good as the fruit of obedience to God. We may think we can't resist temptation, but God has promised us that His divine power has given us everything we need to live a life of radical obedience and self-control." [21] *When we draw on the power of the Holy Spirit, we will experience true strength and fullness.*

Bringing our eating habits under God's control is not an easy process. If we're going to experience victory, we need to think ahead. There are probably certain times in the day or certain places where temptation will be especially strong. We need to plan ahead, having healthy snacks on hand so that it's easier to make the more beneficial choice.

It's also helpful to think ahead to how we will feel after *making a food choice. Sure, junk tastes so good in the moment, but how do we feel after eating it? Are we satisfied? Do we feel stronger? Usually we just feel regret, and often a craving for more of what we just ate.*

---

[21] 2 Peter 1:3

We were created for more. We were created for mission. God has a very specific calling for each one of us, and when we discover it, we'll have taken a gigantic step toward greater fulfillment. Unhealthy food will still be tempting, but the desire for satisfaction will have a new and better outlet.

Ask God to reveal His will for you today. What choice do you need to make in order to eat the food of doing the will of your heavenly Father?

Day Four
FREEDOM THROUGH FASTING

If certain foods or eating habits have a hold on us, then we need something to help us break through to a place of freedom. Fasting is a wonderful spiritual tool that can release God's power and loosen the shackles of irresistible cravings. The practice of fasting flies in the face of a culture that insists that every single desire we feel should be satisfied.

1. What should our motive be when we are fasting? See Zechariah 7:5–6.

We shouldn't fast to mindlessly and heartlessly follow a rule. The purpose of a spiritual fast shouldn't be to lose weight, either. In fasting, as in all things, our motives matter. When we fast, we are getting rid of excess and making space for God. Our focus needs to be on Him, not on the secondary benefits of fasting.

When we fast, a space is created that allows us to hear God better. It gives Him the room to reveal things to us that we desperately need to learn. This benefit of fasting is described by Richard Foster in his book *Celebration of Discipline*:

> More than any other discipline, fasting reveals the things that control us. This is a wonderful benefit to the true disciple who longs to be transformed into the image of Christ. We cover up what is inside us with food and other good things, but in fasting these things surface. If pride controls us, it will be revealed almost immediately. David writes, "I humbled my soul with fasting" (Ps. 69:10). Anger, bitterness, jealousy, strife, fear—if they are within us, they will surface during fasting. At first we will rationalize that our anger is due to our hunger; then we will realize that we are angry because the spirit of anger is

within us. We can rejoice in this knowledge because we know that healing is available through the power of Christ.[22]

2. Another secondary benefit of fasting is greater clarity in prayer as we seek to discern God's will. Although "the purpose of Christian fasting is not to manipulate God into doing what we want, fasting enables us to listen, so we hear God's direction in how to pray."[23] Is there an area of your life where you need God's direction? What is it? Would you consider a fast in order to devote more time to prayer and listening to God's voice?

3. What could you do with the time saved if you spent a day fasting from food? Could you devote that time to prayer?

4. Father Dwight Longenecker wrote regarding fasting, "Through fasting, we gain self-mastery. Limiting our intake of food means we are more self-controlled in other areas of our lives."[24] Do you agree or disagree? Explain.

Quiet your heart and enjoy His presence. . . . It's therapy for the soul.

In the words of Saint John Paul II:

> *Fasting is to reaffirm to oneself what Jesus answered Satan when he tempted him at the end of his 40 days of fasting in the wilderness: "Man shall not live by bread alone but by every word that proceeds from the mouth of God" (Mt 4:4). . . . Today, especially in affluent societies, it is difficult to grasp the meaning of these Gospel words. Consumerism, instead of*

---

[22] Richard J. Foster, *Celebration of Discipline: The Path to Spiritual Growth* (San Francisco: HarperSanFrancisco, 1988), 55.

[23] Lynne Baab, *Fasting: Spiritual Freedom Beyond Our Appetites* (Downers Grove, IL: InterVarsity Press, 2006), 37.

[24] Father Dwight Longenecker, "The Practical Practice of Fasting," *National Catholic Register*, February 13, 2013, http://www.ncregister.com/site/print_article/36265/.

satisfying needs, constantly creates new ones, often generating excessive activism. Everything seems necessary and urgent and one risks not even finding the time to be alone with oneself for a while. . . . Penitential fasting is obviously something very different from a therapeutic diet, but in its own way it can be considered therapy for the soul. In fact practiced as a sign of conversion, it helps one in the interior effort of listening to God.[25]

Fasting helps us to listen to God. As we listen to God, we are living out John 15:5, clinging as a branch to the vine. As we connect to God in this way, He infuses us with what we need to break free from the stranglehold that our cravings can create. We exercise the muscle of self-control and start to experience freedom in ways we never thought possible.

Talk to God about your desire to experience freedom. Tell Him the things that hold you back from fasting. Ask Him to give you His mind and His thoughts on the matter of fasting and to help you to keep your motives pure if you choose to fast in the future.

Day Five
TRULY HUNGRY

1. How often do you experience real hunger in an average week? Do you think it's possible that our tendency to overeat or satisfy every craving deadens our sensitivity to those who are dying of hunger?

2. What do you think of when you pray, "Give us this day our daily bread" in the Our Father? What additional insight do you gain into that petition from CCC 2831?

---

[25] Pope John Paul II, "Penitential Fasting Is Therapy for the Soul," Eternal World Television Network, March 10, 1996, http://www.ewtn.com/library/PAPALDOC/JP960310.HTM.

3. Read Matthew 25:31–46. Where is Christ hidden in this passage?

4. Matthew 25:31–46 teaches that judgment will be tied to the way we have responded to the needs of the poor. How do you feel about the way you have responded to the face of Christ in the poor? How do you feel we respond as a Church? How do you feel we respond as a nation?

Quiet your heart and enjoy His presence. . . . He will awaken your heart to what matters most.

"The way we came to know love was that [Jesus] laid down his life for us; so we ought to lay down our lives for our brothers. If someone who has worldly means sees a brother in need and refuses him compassion, how can the love of God remain in him? Children, let us love not in word or speech but in deed and truth." (1 John 3:16–18)

One way we can lay down our lives for our brothers is by sacrificing some time and money normally devoted to our own food consumption, and feed someone else.

When we seek to be more self-controlled about what we eat, we'll find ourselves asking, "Do I need this food?" It's essential that we distinguish between our needs and wants. When we are willing to set our wants aside, we can start looking beyond ourselves to what we can do for others.

Ask God to reveal to you practical ways that you can set aside your cravings in regard to food, and instead help those who are truly hungry.

Conclusion

It's time for me to pull the disposable casserole trays out of the cupboard. It all started when an elderly deacon in our parish slowly ascended to the podium to tell us that people used to generously make hot dishes for parish volunteers to serve to the homeless on Friday nights, but fewer and fewer were being made now. He pointed to the disposable casserole trays stacked at the back of the church, and pleaded with us to take one home and return it for those in need. I was so moved by his passion that I took two. They sat on the counter all week, crying out to be filled. But I got busy. I was making meals for my own family. I was making cups of tea for myself. I was searching for more sweet treats hidden around the house by my friend. I was getting ready to write a lesson about food. So where was I to find the time? Their emptiness mocked me on the counter, so I put them in the cupboard. Do I get points for not throwing them away? Hmm . . . I'm not so sure.

Do I truly not have time to make a couple of casseroles? What do I normally make time for while my daughter has her piano lesson? That would be a quick trip to Starbucks for some needed (truly needed?) caffeine. Could I forgo this treat and instead spend the time picking up the casserole ingredients? After dinner, instead of watching TV, could I assemble and bake the casseroles? Would it kill me to fast from these two treats today?

There's always a reason to plan to do something tomorrow. We tell ourselves, "I'm just doing the best I can. At some point down the road I'll do xyz, but I just need to get through today." What is the very next choice that you face? How strong is the temptation to make the better choice tomorrow and let today just be a little bit easier?

Are you feeling the way I am, that the time for change is now? If so, don't become overwhelmed by the size of the mountain. Just look at the next choice, and make it the better one. God doesn't give us strength in one big dose. He wants us to come close, and receive the infusion of His self-control and power day by day, moment by moment. When we feel empty, He wants to fill us with Himself. Only He will satisfy. Reach out for Him instead of the cheap substitute, and you won't be disappointed.

My Resolution

In what specific way will I apply what I learned in this lesson?

Examples:

1. This lesson has caused me to recognize that I have put food in a place of importance that should be reserved for God alone. I'll go to confession to ask God's forgiveness so that I can start new patterns with a clean slate and a heart full of grace and strength.

2. I will memorize a Bible verse that reminds me that although I may feel like I can't, with God, I have all the strength and self-control that I need to eat in a way that is truly beneficial to me.

3. I will fast for one day this week, and whenever I feel a hunger pang, I'll take it as a reminder to pray.

My Resolution:

Catechism Clips

CCC 2557 "I want to see God" expresses the true desire of man. Thirst for God is quenched by the water of eternal life (cf. *Jn* 4:14).

CCC 2831 But the presence of those who hunger because they lack bread opens up another profound meaning of this petition. The drama of hunger in the world calls Christians who pray sincerely to exercise responsibility toward their brethren, both in their personal behavior and in their solidarity with the human family. This petition of the Lord's Prayer cannot be isolated from the parables of the poor man Lazarus and of the Last Judgment.

Verse Study

See Appendix 2 for instructions on how to complete a verse study.

Galatians 5:1

1. Verse:

2. Paraphrase:

3. Questions:

4. Cross-references:

5. Personal Application:

Lesson 4

BALANCE THROUGH SELF-DISCIPLINE

Introduction

Self-discipline is absolutely foundational to growing in balance. If we lack this essential trait, our lives will continually be out of kilter. We'll become enslaved to our passions and desires, and easy targets for temptation. Proverbs 25:28 tells us that whoever can't rule over his or her own spirit is like a city broken down, without walls.

Without it, we stay in our cozy beds instead of getting up to pray.
Without it, we skip Mass when Sunday looks too busy.
Without it, we avoid confession like the plague, because we don't like talking about our sins.
Without it, we watch TV or surf the Internet instead of reading the Bible.
Without it, we do what feels fun, comfortable, easy, and relaxing instead of what's good for us.
Without it, our thoughts run wild and the worries of tomorrow rob today of its joy.

Self-discipline is like a muscle that is built up by many small decisions to say no to what we feel like doing or thinking, and yes to what we know is best and right. Exercising self-discipline strengthens the intellect so it can rule over the will.

Focusing on self-discipline is not without pitfalls, however. As we grow in our ability to make decisions based on what we know to be right instead of what we feel like doing, we'll be tempted to credit ourselves with this progress. This is the fatal mistake of thinking that all we've accomplished has been due to our own strength and ability. This was the error made by a British monk named Pelagius (AD 354–420), who denied original sin and insisted that if a man knew what was good, he could become self-disciplined through sheer determination. Pelagius was denounced as a heretic at the Council of Carthage (AD 418). Vestiges of this heresy remain in our belief that all we need to live a self-disciplined life is willpower. Nothing could be further from the truth. Any progress we make is due to God's work in us. Self-help books that leave God out of the picture fall into this trap.

Another pitfall is to view self-discipline as an end in itself. Self-discipline is not the goal of the Christian life. Our goal is growing in our relationship with Christ and becoming more like Him.

God wants to work within us to make us holy, but He won't force Himself on us. Self-discipline gets us into a position of opening our hearts to God's power and strength so that He can work in and through us. It's my prayer that we'll grow in self-discipline, making the small decisions that will put us in a position for God to accomplish in us far more than we could ask or imagine.

Day One
THE GIFT OF SELF-DISCIPLINE

1. What has God given each one of His children, according to 2 Timothy 1:7?

Self-discipline, or self-control, is a gift from God. It's one of the fruits of the Holy Spirit (see Galatians 5:22), placed within us through grace. It's an unearned gift, given by the most generous Father.

2. How would you describe the relationship between our own effort and God's power in the development of self-discipline? See Colossians 1:29. Reading this verse in multiple versions of the Bible can give added insight into its meaning (see biblehub.com).

"Not by might, and not by power, but by my spirit, says the Lord." (Zechariah 4:6)

3. Self-discipline is required if we're going to live the Christian life victoriously. The alternative is living a life of defeat, trapped in patterns of bad behavior. Many people are able to change bad habits through sheer determination and grit. This is not what we're talking about in this lesson. What is one way we can check

ourselves to make sure that we are progressing in the Christian life by relying on *God's* power and not our own? See Proverbs 21:31.

Author Ken Boa has this to say about self-discipline:

> Many people think self-discipline is simply a matter of trying harder. Yet the Bible speaks of self-discipline as a fruit of the Spirit. Plants don't produce more fruit by trying harder. Transformation is the work of God done with our cooperation. God supplies the power, but there is a direct correlation between the amount of transformation taking place and the types of activities a follower of Christ engages in. . . . This is how spiritual transformation works. Discipline and dependence go hand in hand. We can pursue it, but we can take no credit for it.[26]

Quiet your heart and enjoy His presence. . . . Connect to the source and be filled with His grace.

Prayerfully reflect on how far you have come spiritually since you first encountered Christ. Do you see evidence of the ways that He has strengthened and empowered you to grow spiritually? Thank Him for the gift of self-discipline. Ask Him to shed light on any areas of your life where you are tempted to say, "I can't!" Read 2 Timothy 1:7 in light of that situation, asking God to help you draw on the power and self-control that He has placed within you.

Day Two
THE MOTIVATION FOR GROWING IN SELF-DISCIPLINE

What is the motivation for self-discipline? We need it to mature spiritually. The story is told of a teacher who applied for a promotion after twenty-five years in the classroom. She was passed over for a teacher with only one year of experience. Frustrated, she asked the principal why. The principal replied, "You haven't actually had twenty-five years of experience, as you claimed. You've actually had only one year of experience twenty-five times." In all those years, the teacher had not improved. Sadly, the same thing can often be said for many Christians. Just because we've sat in

---

[26] Kenneth Boa, "Self-Discipline," Bible.org, November 2, 2005, https://bible.org/seriespage/self-discipline.

the pew or read the Bible for years doesn't mean we're maturing. We might just be repeating the same lessons over and over without growth.

1. What was frustrating for the author of Hebrews as he endeavored to teach his readers spiritual truth? See Hebrews 5:11–14.

2. It was difficult for the writer of Hebrews to lead his readers to a place of spiritual maturity because they had "become sluggish in hearing." (verse 11) Perhaps the truth seemed boring. Maybe they were feeling apathetic toward their faith. This sluggishness put them in a dangerous position. What is at risk when people become "sluggish in hearing"? See 2 Timothy 4:3–4.

It takes self-discipline to choose to expose ourselves to the meat of truth, instead of seeking to be entertained.

3. A diet of milk is necessary for a baby. In that same way, someone new to his or her faith needs to be taught the basics. The author of Hebrews was talking to people who needed to progress and graduate to solid food. According to 5:12, what did the writer of Hebrews feel his readers should be doing by this point?

While we all will not have equal teaching ability, all Christians should be able to pass on their faith. Everyone who has encountered Christ in a life-changing way has something to share. When we do nothing because we can't figure out what to say, we are missing an opportunity to grow. If we step out and share the difference Christ has made in our lives, we will be stretched and matured. Sometimes we'll make mistakes, which we'll learn from, and that's OK. What's not OK is to not bother trying.

4. We will stagnate in the spiritual life if we fail to apply the lessons we have been taught. Is there a lesson God has taught you, but you have failed to apply to your life? What is something specific you can do to discipline yourself to act on that lesson? Can you commit to *do it now*, instead of putting it off for later?

Quiet your heart and enjoy His presence. . . . We grow as we seek His face.

We all want to be mature. If that weren't the case, we wouldn't be doing this Bible study! But wanting maturity and growing in maturity are two different things. Ask God to shed light on areas of spiritual immaturity in your life. Ask Him to help you to desire the truth, even when it isn't what you want to hear. Ask Him for an appetite for meat, even though entertainment is temporarily satisfying. Remember, He never leaves us to climb the hill of spiritual maturity alone. Picture a young girl standing on her father's feet while dancing. This is what God invites us to do. He'll do the real work, but we need to take His hands and step onto His feet. With our gaze on Him, He'll equip us with all we need to progress on the path to maturity.

Day Three
HOW TO GROW IN SELF-DISCIPLINE

Read 1 Corinthians 9:24–27.

1. What is required of an athlete if she is going to "run so as to win"? What would be the consequence of her just making an effort once in a while? Do you see parallels between the discipline needed to progress athletically and that needed to progress spiritually?

2. An athlete disciplines herself in order to "win a perishable crown." As Christians, what are we disciplining ourselves to win? See 1 Corinthians 9:25.

3. Before setting the goal of winning a race, an athlete has to determine if the prize is worth the cost. The same is true for Christians. Is the reward of seeing God face-to-face worth it? What sacrifices are you willing to make today in order to receive this prize?

Growing in self-discipline starts with little decisions that have big consequences. Developing the following habits strengthens our ability to make those smart choices.

- Do the hard things first. Procrastination is a barrier to self-discipline. Force yourself to set aside the pleasurable (often lower-priority) tasks and get the tough stuff out of the way.

- Be on time. When we're rushing around, we're more apt to make decisions based on convenience rather than what is wisest or best.

- Follow through. Strive to finish whatever project you start. Switch-tasking (switching back and forth between two tasks) will get in the way of this goal. It's inefficient and often means that two tasks are done halfway instead of one being done thoroughly.

- Be faithful to your word. This requires being careful about what you commit to. Before making the commitment, carefully consider what your yes will involve. Do you have what it takes to follow through and be faithful to your word?

- Keep your eye on the goal. Nothing gets in the way of this like our desire to be entertained. Let entertainment be your reward for a job well done, not the one thing in your day you refuse to give up.

4. Which of the habits listed above do you find most challenging? Can you see evidence of the way your struggle in this area makes being self-disciplined more difficult?

Quiet your heart and enjoy His presence. . . . Look at life from God's perspective.

"I have competed well; I have finished the race; I have kept the faith. From now on the crown of righteousness awaits me, which the Lord, the just judge, will award to me on that day, and not only to me, but to all who have longed for his appearance." (2 Timothy 4:7–8)

When Saint Paul wrote the words above, he was facing death. The way he had lived prepared him for a beautiful eternity. His life was the compilation of countless small decisions—decisions to do what he knew to be right even if it didn't feel good in the moment. He lived purposefully, knowing that his time on earth was so short compared to eternity. Any pain on earth was worth his heavenly reward.

Spend a few moments talking to God about eternity. Ask Him to give you insight into how your decisions today are preparing you for heaven.

Day Four
SELF-DISCIPLINE AND SPIRITUAL NOURISHMENT

If we aren't getting spiritual nourishment, we won't be able to "run so as to win" (1 Corinthians 9:24) or "finish the race." (2 Timothy 4:7) Just as an athlete won't make much progress if she is inconsistent with her training, our progress depends on how we are nourished on a *daily* basis.

1. After the Old Testament Israelites had been freed from slavery in Egypt, God began to lead them toward their inheritance in the Promised Land. During the journey, the Israelites became hungry. What did God provide for them to eat, and specifically how and when did He want the Israelites to gather it? See Exodus 16:4–6.

2. What happened if the Israelites tried to gather extra one day in order to eat it the following day? See Exodus 16:16–20.

3. According to CCC 2837, what is *our* daily bread from heaven? (Skim the first paragraph; the answer is found in the second paragraph.)

4. Are you being spiritually nourished *daily*, or are you trying to gather up enough one day a week to last through the following days? Can you see evidence that gathering one day doesn't prove sufficient for the next?

Quiet your heart and enjoy His presence. . . . He longs to nourish you every day.

It takes self-discipline to go to Christ for daily *spiritual nourishment. It might seem more efficient to just load up with spiritual mojo once a week, but it simply doesn't work. It doesn't give you what you need to go the distance. Pray the Our Father, paying special attention to the words "Give us this day our daily bread." What does that mean spiritually? Reflect on those words. Jesus waits every day to nourish you. Do you have the self-discipline to make the decision to go and receive what He offers?*

Day Five
THE COST OF SELF-DISCIPLINE

Gary Player, an incredibly successful international golfer, had lost count of how many times someone said to him, "I'd give anything if I could hit a golf ball like you." He usually gave a polite thank-you and moved on. But on a particularly hard day, he gave the more candid reply, "No, you wouldn't. You'd give anything to hit a golf ball like me, if it were easy." He then went on to explain the cost behind his success: "You've got to get up at five o'clock in the morning, go out and hit a thousand golf balls, walk up to the club house to put a bandage on your hand where it started bleeding, then go and hit another thousand golf balls. That's what it takes to hit a golf ball like me."[27]

How often do we do the same in the spiritual life? We look at someone who is a spiritual giant in our eyes, and wish that we'd had her parents, or her advantages, or her knowledge. What we fail to see is the many small decisions she's made in secret that have cost her something. We see the end result. The saint knows the sacrifice that got her there.

1. *Why* we pursue greater spiritual depth has an enormous impact on whether or not we'll be willing to pay the price to get there. Do you want Jesus in your life in order to feel better when you think about deeper issues and eternity? Do you want just enough of Jesus to make you feel good, but not so much that you have to make radical changes? How do you tend to react when following Jesus involves sacrifice?

2. Read Luke 9:57–62. In this passage, all three people wanted to follow Jesus. But what did they *not* want?

3. Think of a specific area of your life where you need to grow in self-discipline. You know what God is asking of you, and you know that saying yes is going to cost you something. How are you responding? All too often, we say, "Yes, God, I want to follow you and obey you in that specific area of my life, but . . ." And then we insert some qualification that lessens our degree of commitment. What is your yes-but?

---

[27] James Emery White, *You Can Experience . . . A Spiritual Life* (Nashville, TN: Word Publishing, 1999), 201.

4. In Luke 9:23, Jesus summarized the cost of following Him. What does that verse mean to you?

Quiet your heart and enjoy His presence. . . . He has held nothing back from you.

Jesus waits to spend time with us every morning. He recognizes that taking up our cross each day is costly. Because He never wants us to try to bear its weight with our own strength, He offers us His resurrection power (Ephesians 1:19–20). It's up to us to ask for it, though.

As we come to Him in prayer, Jesus asks us to cross the line between a life of casual commitment to Him, and one in which we offer Him everything. He asks us to hold nothing back. He asks us to count the cost, and to consider Him worth everything. Talk to Him about your desire to follow Him. Ask Him to give you the strength and power to relinquish your yes-but. He's asking for your undivided heart.

Conclusion

"Do you also want to leave?" John 6:67

When Jesus told His followers that unless they ate His flesh and drank His blood they had no eternal life in them, many of them "no longer accompanied him." (John 6:66) What He was asking them to accept was a little too much. It was too radical. They didn't necessarily walk away from Him and toward a life of depravity. They just went back to what was considered normal. As a result, they missed living the life they were created for.

Do you also want to go away? Do you feel tempted to do the "slow fade," in which you take little steps away from the Lord when what He asks seems too much?

The call to follow Christ requires self-discipline. It means laying aside what we feel like doing in order to do what God has said is right. And it's costly. Following Christ means entering into a mutually self-giving relationship. There's nothing casual about it. It's an intimacy that grows as we say, "I want what you want, when you want it, how you want it," and then act on that commitment.

But may we never make the mistake of thinking this is accomplished through pure willpower—gritting our teeth and powering through. The obedience of self-discipline is brought about through our surrender to the Holy Spirit. He does in and through us what we can't do ourselves. When we pray, "Give me the strength to do what I know is right even though I don't feel like it," the Holy Spirit comes through for us.

This was Saint Teresa of Calcutta's secret. Early in her life, she made a pact with God to refuse Him nothing. She said, "If God imparts himself fully to us, shall we answer with just a fraction of ourselves?"[28] She determined to "do His bidding without delay" and "to be found faithful in the little practices." And what resulted from her Spirit-fueled self-discipline? The world was changed, one heart at a time. There is no limit to what God can do in and through a woman who has this kind of relationship with Him.

My Resolution

In what specific way will I apply what I learned in this lesson?

Examples:

1. I will exercise self-discipline by setting my alarm early enough to get up and pray—and I'll get up when the alarm goes off. I'll remember that prayerlessness means heading into the day relying on myself instead of being filled with God's strength and power.

2. When I look at my calendar or to-do list for the day, I'll determine to do the hardest things first.

3. When I go forward for the Eucharist, I will prayerfully place on the altar my yes-but. I'll ask God to fill me with His strength and power to leave it on the altar. When I return to the pew and kneel to pray, I'll ask Him for the strength to "refuse Him nothing."

---

[28] Mother Teresa, *Mother Teresa: Come Be My Light: The Private Writings of the Saint of Calcutta*, ed. Brian Kolodiejchuk (New York: Doubleday, 2007), 29.

My Resolution:

Catechism Clips

CCC 2837 "Daily" (*epiousios*) occurs nowhere else in the New Testament. Taken in a temporal sense, this word is a pedagogical repetition of "this day," to confirm us in trust "without reservation." Taken in the qualitative sense, it signifies what is necessary for life, and more broadly every good thing sufficient for subsistence. Taken literally (*epi-ousios*: "super-essential"), it refers directly to the Bread of Life, the Body of Christ, the "medicine of immortality," without which we have no life within us. Finally in this connection, its heavenly meaning is evident: "this day" is the Day of the Lord, the day of the feast of the kingdom, anticipated in the Eucharist that is already the foretaste of the kingdom to come. For this reason it is fitting for the Eucharistic liturgy to be celebrated each day.

> The Eucharist is our daily bread. The power belonging to this divine food makes it a bond of union. Its effect is then understood as unity, so that, gathered into his Body and made members of him, we may become what we receive. . . . This also is our daily bread: the readings you hear each day in church and the hymns you hear and sing. All these are necessities for our pilgrimage.

> The Father in heaven urges us, as children of heaven, to ask for the bread of heaven. [Christ] himself is the bread who, sown in the Virgin, raised up in the flesh, kneaded in the Passion, baked in the oven of the tomb, reserved in churches, brought to altars, furnishes the faithful each day with food from heaven.

Verse Study

See Appendix 2 for instructions on how to complete a verse study.

Matthew 7:21

1. Verse:

2. Paraphrase:

3. Questions:

4. Cross-references:

5. Personal Application:

NOTES

Lesson 5

BALANCE THROUGH ENGAGING CULTURE

Introduction

Once we decide to take our relationship with Christ seriously, it isn't long before we find ourselves in the messy land of trying to figure out how we should relate to the culture around us. We don't want to seem weird. We'd rather not offend people with our different values. At the same time, we don't want to compromise what God says matters most. It's complicated further by the fact that we're not just wrestling with our positions on certain "issues." We're relating to real people whom we love. We want to show the difference that Christ makes, but in the words of author Alvin Reid, not in an "odd-for-God" kind of way.

We read John 3:16, "For God so loved the world that he gave his only Son, so that everyone who believes in him might not perish but might have eternal life." God loves the world. Therefore, we should love the world. Easy enough.

But then we read 1 John 2:15, "Do not love the world or the things of the world. If anyone loves the world, the love of the Father is not in him." What?! Aren't we supposed to *love* the world?

We read 2 Corinthians 6:17, "'Therefore, come out from them and be separate,' says the Lord, 'and touch nothing unclean; then I will receive you.'" I guess this means we'd better eat only at Chick-fil-A (it's owned by Christians) or at home.

But then we read Mark 16:15, "[Jesus] said to them, 'Go into the whole world and proclaim the gospel to every creature.'" Hmm . . . this will be a little bit difficult to do if we're so separate that everyone we talk to already believes what we believe.

So it's no wonder that we find it all a bit tricky to navigate. And while we try to figure out how to live authentic Christian lives without conforming to the wrong things, people in our neighborhoods, in our families, in our schools, at our workplaces, and in our communities continue to look for something different; something that makes sense of things; something that is bigger than the best Oprah's got to offer. They are longing for the transcendent. They are looking for God.

How do we demonstrate Christ to the world? Should we blend in? Should we stand out? How do we live out our faith in a culture where Christians are better known for what they are against than what they are for?

Let's jump into the murkiness and ask God to shine His light to guide us.

Day One
THE PROBLEM OF "US" VERSUS "THEM"

1. A. What do you believe are the biggest problems within contemporary culture?

   B. Reflect on your answer. How many of the problems listed have to do with sin that can be found within your own heart?

2. A common response to the moral decay observed in the culture is to see the main problem as "out there" as opposed to "in here," in our own hearts. This leads to an "us" versus "them" mentality. From this perspective, the purity of "us" must be protected and preserved, and the sin of "them" is to be separated and pointed out. In his book *The Gulag Archipelago*, Aleksandr Solzhenitsyn explains why he believes this is a problematic way of looking at life:

   > If only it were all so simple! If only there were evil people somewhere insidiously committing evil deeds, and it were necessary only to separate them from the rest of us and destroy them. But the line dividing good and evil cuts through the heart of every human being. And who is willing to destroy a piece of his own heart?[29]

---

[29] Aleksandr Solzhenitsyn, *The Gulag Archipelago* (New York: The Harvill Press, 1974), 442.

Think about Solzhenitsyn's words. Do you agree or disagree? Share your thoughts.

3. What is Jesus' response to the "us" versus "them" mentality? See Matthew 7:1–5.

4. Fear often lurks behind judgment. One of the reasons Christians have become better known for what they are against than what they are for is because we are afraid of truth being compromised. We want to defend the Church. We are afraid that if we don't speak loudly about what is wrong, the dark side will win. What did Jesus say to Peter about the strength of the Church? See Matthew 16:18.

God doesn't need our protection. He is far greater than that. The chief objective of the Church is not self-preservation. This is not to be our concern, because Jesus has promised us that God will always do a good job of protecting the Church. In other words, we aren't allowed to ignore His command in Matthew 7 (Don't judge) in the name of fighting on His behalf.

This is not to say that there is no place for our voices to speak truth within the culture. But the way in which we do it really matters, as does the motive behind our words. (Does it come from compassion for those who need Jesus or fear of them and their influence?)

Quiet your heart and enjoy His presence. . . . Go before the Throne of Grace on behalf of those who need God's love.

In his book They Like Jesus but Not the Church, *Dan Kimball describes what happens to Christians who love Jesus but retreat into a bubble, into a Christian subculture. He says that we begin to relate to the secular culture in the same way that Jonah related to Nineveh when God called him to go and preach to its people. Jonah didn't want to go. He didn't feel they deserved God's grace. Jonah related to Nineveh by complaining about it.[30]*

How much time do we spend praying for the people we are tempted to judge? Are we more likely to pray for them or to pity them?

We started today's lesson by listing problems we see in our culture. Spend some time in compassionate prayer for the people behind those issues.

Day Two
PUT THE STONES DOWN

Read John 8:1–11.

1. Describe the scene through the eyes of the woman caught in adultery. What did she see? Where did they make her stand? If you could choose just one word to describe how she felt, what would it be?

2. When the scribes and Pharisees asked Jesus if He thought the woman should be stoned, He bent down and began to write on the ground with His finger. After making them wait, how did Jesus finally answer them? How did the scribes and Pharisees respond?

---

[30] Dan Kimball, *They Like Jesus but Not the Church* (Grand Rapids, MI: Zondervan, 2007), 45.

3. Who are the people who are often "made to stand in the middle" of Christians' judgment? We may not physically drag a person into our presence, but we circle him or her with the judgment of our words, written and spoken. (Note that the question is not about whom the Church judges. It's about whom *we* judge.)

4. All too often, we don't realize the way we are making people feel. It's hard to see things from another person's perspective, especially when we are so busy all the time. Writer and speaker Sibi Riffer describes what it felt like for her to come to church as an unwed mother with a baby on her hip:

> I can remember pulling into church parking lots again and again and sitting there bawling my eyes out as I watched married couple after married couple walk inside the holy doors of *we have it all together—sorry about your luck.*
>
> I never had the courage to actually go inside.
>
> Then finally, I can remember it taking everything I had to walk in those dreaded doors one Sunday morning with my baby girl in my arms. I was an unwed single mama raising a baby on about $6.00 an hour and no support of any kind. I left the trailer that morning and looked at the gift that I didn't deserve and told her we were going to give this Jesus a try. I cried the entire way there and wondered if I looked nice enough, good enough, clean enough, churchy-enough.
>
> I wondered if all of the perfect people would be able to see me past the missing wedding ring and the beautiful baby girl on my hip.
>
> I wondered if they would embrace me. Accept me. Allow me in—in spite of my circumstances and in spite of my mistakes.
>
> I'm sorry to share that I walked into a sea of judgment and condemnation during that season of my life.
>
> And unfortunately it caused me to leave the church for nearly a decade.

Because when you are struggling with the lie that is "there is no way that a holy God could love a girl like me." And you are hanging on by a thread because life has just been too much . . .

Every moment counts.

The way you are received and welcomed or not.

The way the caregivers receive your child with kindness or not.

The way a seat is made available for you or not.

The way you are looked down upon, questioned or *interrogated* by church members or *hopefully not.*

The way someone took the time to speak with you or not.

The way you are shamed and condemned or accepted and loved.

All of those things and so much more are some of the reasons that people will give church and ultimately Jesus another chance.

But one of the biggest reasons I walked away was this. *I didn't want what they had.*

They made it loud and clear to me what they were against.

But they failed to demonstrate what they were for.[31]

Intentionally or unintentionally, we can shame and condemn the very people Jesus wants us to reach out to with love. What are practical ways we can lovingly lead other women to Christ?

---

[31] "The New Church Lady," *Pearls and Grace* (blog), February 6, 2014, http://pearlsandgrace.blogspot.com/2014/01/the-new-church-lady.html.

Quiet your heart and enjoy His presence. . . . Let His kindness and gentleness fill you so you can pass it on to others.

"So we are ambassadors for Christ, as if God were appealing through us." (2 Corinthians 5:20)

It's time for us to put down our stones. In a world that seeks to objectify women, we need to come alongside one another. Instead of judging one another, let's lead each other to Christ. Let's leave it to Him to point out the sin. He can be trusted to do this! Remember, He never condoned the adulterous woman's behavior. He said, "Go, and from now on do not sin any more." (John 8:11) We don't have to worry that if we stop shouting through our megaphones about what's sinful, humanity will go over the edge into the abyss. God can be trusted to convict people of sin. That's a big part of the Holy Spirit's job. But it's not our job. God's voice can be heard through gentle truth-tellers. Ask God to reveal to you which stone is in your hand. Ask Him for the grace to put it down and instead offer love and mercy.

Day Three
EARNING THE RIGHT TO BE HEARD

Earning the right to be heard is critical if we're going to engage our culture and draw others closer to Christ. One way to do this is to build genuine relationships with people instead of treating them as "projects" in need of improvement. Another is to live in such a way that we earn people's respect and trust.

Sometimes we mistakenly think that we have to be in full-time ministry in order to really make a difference in the world for Christ. Nothing could be further from the truth. The issue isn't what job we are doing. The issue is *how* we live out our vocations, whether we're at home, in business, in politics, or anywhere else. In the words of Pope Francis, "Missionary fervor does not require extraordinary events. It is in ordinary life that mission work is done."

We can be engaged in tasks that don't seem to have anything to do with our faith. But what's going on *within* us should make us distinct. According to theologian John Frame, the difference should be found in the "motive, goal and standard" behind our work.[32]

---

[32] John M. Frame, *The Doctrine of the Christian Life* (Phillipsburg, NJ: P&R Publishing, 2008), 874.

When our motives, goals, and standards are right, we are living lives of integrity. This earns us the right to be heard. This causes us to stand out in the crowd, and gives weight to our message.

1. What do the following verses teach us in terms of the motives, goals, and standards that should be seen in our lives? See Matthew 5:41, 1 Corinthians 10:31, Colossians 3:23.

2. Pope Francis said, "When leaders in various fields ask me for advice, my response is always the same: dialogue, dialogue, dialogue. It is the only way for individuals, families, and societies to grow, the only way for the life of peoples to progress, along with the culture of encounter, a culture in which all have something good to give and all can receive something good in return. Others always have something to give me, if we know how to approach them in a spirit of openness and without prejudice." How can you apply his advice to your own life?

The late Chuck Colson, founder of Prison Fellowship, described it this way:

> We must enter into the stories of the surrounding culture, which takes real listening. . . . We connect with the literature, music, theater, arts, and issues that express the existing culture's hopes, dreams, and fears. This builds a bridge by which we can show how the gospel can enter and transform those stories.[33]

3. What insights do you gain from Colossians 4:5–6 and 1 Peter 3:15–16 in terms of whether or not we should share our faith and in what manner?

---

[33] Charles Colson and Ellen Vaughn, *Being the Body* (Nashville, TN: W Publishing, 2003), 371.

4. Earning the right to be heard requires living a life of integrity (having the right motive, goal, and standard), listening before speaking, and sharing your views with graciousness, gentleness, and reverence. In which of these areas do you most want to grow?

Quiet your heart and enjoy His presence. . . . Let Him fill you with His words.

"If we, each doing our own part, if we do good to others, if we meet there, doing good, and we go slowly, gently, little by little, we will make that culture of encounter: we need that so much. We must meet one another doing good." —Pope Francis

It isn't easy to listen when we are so certain that what we have to say will help. And sometimes it's hard to articulate what we believe, let alone to do it graciously and gently. God wants to help us. When we don't know what to say or how to say it, He wants us to call upon the Holy Spirit. When Jesus was speaking to the disciples about this very issue, He told them, "Do not worry about how you are to speak or what you are to say. You will be given at that moment what you are to say. For it will not be you who speak but the Spirit of your Father speaking through you." (Matthew 10:19– 20) Which of your upcoming conversations needs to be sprinkled with salt? Ask God to speak through you.

Day Four
IN THE WORLD BUT DISTINCT

1. Is cultural withdrawal an option for Christians if they are going to be obedient to Christ? See Matthew 28:19–20.

"We need to avoid the spiritual sickness of a church that is wrapped up in its own world: when a church becomes like this, it grows sick. It is true that going out on to the street implies the risk of accidents happening, as they would to any ordinary man or woman. But if the church stays wrapped up in itself, it will age. And if I had to choose between a wounded church that goes out on to the streets and a sick, withdrawn church, I would definitely choose the first one." —Pope Francis

2. What did Jesus say might result if we speak about our faith in Him? See Matthew 5:11.

3. Do you believe that being popular with everyone indicates compromise? Is it possible to fit in too much?

4. When evangelist D. L. Moody was asked to explain the relationship between the Church and the world, he replied, "The place for the ship is in the sea; but God help the ship if the sea gets into it." What do you think it means to be in the world but not of it? See John 17:14–19.

In his book *Unfashionable: Making a Difference in the World by Being Different*, author Tullian Tchividjian shares his take on this passage of Scripture:

> Christ has called his followers to be in the world yet distinct from it, to live against the world, for the world. The truth is, if you follow Jesus in this way, you will seem "too pagan for your Christian friends and too Christian for your pagan friends."[34]

---

[34] Tullian Tchividjian, *Unfashionable: Making a Difference in the World by Being Different* (Colorado Springs: Multnomah Books, 2012), 82.

Quiet your heart and enjoy His presence. . . . You don't have to think about how to act with Him. Just be.

Dear Lord,

It's uncomfortable to follow you.

When I'm obedient to you, I sometimes feel that I don't fit in anywhere. There can be an element of loneliness in faithfulness.

Help me to remember that this earth isn't my home; heaven is. That's where I truly belong—with you. When I feel I don't blend in here, may it remind me that I was made for more. That more is eternity. Help me to remember that the goal of my life isn't being comfortable or happy. Help me to persevere with whatever you are asking, even if it seems like no matter what I do, someone is unhappy with me. Help me to remember that it's a real gift that I can just be with you. It's not a performance. You just want the real me.

Day Five
FEARLESSLY POSITIVE

1. No one is drawn to negativity. It indicates a lack of hope, which is truly the opposite of the message of the gospel. According to CCC 2527, what does the gospel (the Good News of Christ) have the power to do?

2. In what ways can Christians reveal the power of the gospel by *restoring* culture with a fearlessly positive spirit? Think of the different aspects of culture (film, literature, art, music, fashion, etc.). What might happen if Christians *stepped into* the aspects of culture that they typically back away from and criticize?

3. Author Austen Ivereigh has this to say about the positive manner in which we should engage culture:

> Being positive is not about smiling and being "nice." It is about bringing the discussion back to the positive vision the Church has for people—the endless, wonderful possibilities of our freedom. Catholic Voices should be idealists and radicals, inviting society to another, better way. Pro-Lifers should sound like anti-slavery campaigners, not admonishing moralists, just as opponents of assisted dying should be campaigners for hospices on every corner. Don't be a grim reaper; be the angel that points to the brighter horizon.[35]

How would you describe "the positive vision the Church has for people—the endless, wonderful possibilities of our freedom"? What hope and goodness does the Church offer the world?

4. A negative outlook on the world can indicate a lack of confidence in Christ's power to overcome obstacles. Pope Francis addresses this in his encyclical *The Joy of the Gospel (Evangelii Gaudium)*:

> One of the most serious temptations which stifles boldness and zeal is a defeatism which turns us into querulous and disillusioned pessimists, "sourpusses." Nobody can go off to battle unless he is fully convinced of victory beforehand. If we start without confidence, we have already lost half the battle and we bury our talents. While painfully aware of our own frailties, we have to march on without giving in, keeping in mind what the Lord said to Saint Paul: "My grace is sufficient for you, for my power is made perfect in weakness" (2 Cor 12:9). Christian triumph is always a cross, yet a cross which is at the same time a victorious banner borne with aggressive tenderness against the assaults of evil. The evil spirit of defeatism is brother to the temptation to separate, before its time, the wheat from the weeds; it is the fruit of an anxious and self-centered lack of trust.[36]

---

[35] Austen Ivereigh, How to Defend the Faith Without Raising Your Voice: Civil Responses to Catholic Hot Button Issues (Huntington, IN: Our Sunday Visitor Publishing Division, 2012), 156.

[36] Pope Francis, *The Joy of the Gospel* (Dublin, Ireland: Veritas Publications, 2013), 50.

Answer the following questions based on this section of the encyclical.

A. What does Pope Francis say stifles boldness and zeal?

B. What happens if we start into battle with no confidence in the future victory?

C. What do we need to remember when we are aware of our own frailties?

Quiet your heart and enjoy His presence. . . . Regain your fearless positivity as you focus on God's greatness and indomitable love.

We can be fully confident that no matter how bad things get, God will have the victory in the end. He has already won the battle against sin and death!

Prayerfully read the following paraphrase of Saint Paul's words in Romans 8:31–39, and return to them anytime you feel evil is getting the upper hand.

> *So, what do you think? With God on our side like this, how can we lose? If God didn't hesitate to put everything on the line for us, embracing our condition and exposing himself to the worst by sending his own Son, is there anything else he wouldn't gladly and freely do for us? And who would dare tangle with God by messing with one of God's chosen? Who would dare even to point a finger? The One who died for us—who was raised to life for us!—is in the presence of God at this very moment sticking up for us. Do you think anyone is going to be able to drive a wedge between us and Christ's love for us? There is no way! Not trouble, not hard times, not hatred, not hunger, not homelessness, not bullying threats, not backstabbing, not even the worst sins listed in Scripture. . . .*

None of this fazes us because Jesus loves us. I'm absolutely convinced that nothing—nothing living or dead, angelic or demonic, today or tomorrow, high or low, thinkable or unthinkable—absolutely nothing can get between us and God's love because of the way that Jesus our Master has embraced us.[37]

"In all these things, we conquer overwhelmingly through him who loved us." (Romans 8:37)

Conclusion

We have countless opportunities to talk with people whose opinions differ from ours. How do we interact with them? Are we gracious or judgmental? Do we listen to or talk at people? Do we treat those who are different as "them" and thank God that we are "us"?

There is so much at stake. A cultural retreat into a Christian bubble is not an option. This means we have got to learn how to communicate winsomely with people who believe differently than we do. This doesn't mean that we compromise or blend in. It means we engage in a positive way that invites dialogue. *Dialogue.* This is going to require listening. All too often, when we "listen" we are actually preparing to make our next point. People can sense this, and it usually shuts down the discussion pretty fast.

I think it would make a big difference if we started saying things like, "Please tell me more about that." Or, "I don't know, let me give that some thought and come back to discuss it later." Or, "I'd really like to learn from you in this way." People rarely remember our arguments, but they always remember if they felt respected or belittled in our presence.

It's always a help when we continuously look for ways we can create a *connection* to people with whom we disagree. Although we might have a very different way in which we feel the dignity of life should be protected, it's possible that a bridge can be built by discussing our mutual desire to see people experience freedom, respect and dignity. We can search for values that we share with others and build on that.

If the person we are talking to begins to get heated and defensive, it's worth at least considering the possibility that his or her reaction may be related to a trigger– a painful event previously experienced. We have the opportunity to love and listen

---

[37] "Romans 8:31–39 (The Message)," Bible Gateway, accessed February 26, 2014, http://www.biblegateway.com/passage/?search=Romans+8%3A31-39&version=MSG.

compassionately. This will be remembered far longer and more positively than us managing to get a couple more of our points made.

The truth is, people remember a story far better than an argument. Any time we can simply share the difference that Christ has made in our lives, walls tend to come down. It's hard to argue with someone's personal experience.

If you want to learn more about civil communication, I highly recommend Austen Ivereigh's book *How to Defend the Faith Without Raising Your Voice*. There's too much at stake for us to keep winging it. It's time for us to educate ourselves in terms of meeting people in the middle, with both truth and love.

"This is how all will know that you are my disciples, if you have love for one another." (John 13:35)

My Resolution

In what specific way will I apply what I learned in this lesson?

Examples:

1. I'll go to confession to ask forgiveness for the times lately that I've thrown stones at others with my thoughts, words, or actions.

2. I'll get together with someone who I know has a different set of beliefs than I do. My objective during our time together will simply be to listen and to get to know him or her better.

3. At the end of each day, I'll check whether or not my communication with others has been fearlessly positive. Have I fallen into the habit of negativity? If so, I'll confess it, and determine to be a positive representative of Jesus' joy tomorrow.

My Resolution:

Catechism Clips

CCC 2527 "The Good News of Christ continually renews the life and culture of fallen man; it combats and removes the error and evil which flow from the ever-present attraction of sin. It never ceases to purify and elevate the morality of peoples. It takes the spiritual qualities and endowments of every age and nation, and with supernatural riches it causes them to blossom, as it were, from within; it fortifies, completes, and restores them in Christ."

Verse Study

See Appendix 2 for instructions on how to complete a verse study.

Philippians 4:8

1. Verse:

2. Paraphrase:

3. Questions:

4. Cross-references:

5. Personal Application:

NOTES

Appendices

NOTES

Appendix 1
SAINT THÉRÈSE OF LISIEUX

Patron Saint of Walking with Purpose

Saint Thérèse of Lisieux was gifted with the ability to take the riches of our Catholic faith and explain them in a way that a child could imitate. The wisdom she gleaned from Scripture ignited a love in her heart for her Lord that was personal and transforming. The simplicity of the faith that she laid out in her writings is so completely Catholic that Pope Pius XII said, "She rediscovered the Gospel itself, the very heart of the Gospel."

Walking with Purpose is intended to be a means by which women can honestly share their spiritual struggles and embark on a journey that is refreshing to the soul. It was never intended to facilitate the deepest of intellectual study of Scripture. Instead, the focus has been to help women know Christ: to know His heart, to know His tenderness, to know His mercy, and to know His love. Our logo is a little flower, and that has meaning. When a woman begins to open her heart to God, it's like the opening of a little flower. It can easily be bruised or crushed, and it must be treated with the greatest of care. Our desire is to speak to women's hearts no matter where they are in life, baggage and all, and gently introduce truths that can change their lives.

Saint Thérèse of Lisieux, the little flower, called her doctrine "the little way of spiritual childhood," and it is based on complete and unshakable confidence in God's love for us. She was not introducing new truths. She spent countless hours reading Scripture and she shared what she found, emphasizing the importance of truths that had already been divinely revealed. We can learn so much from her:

> The good God would not inspire unattainable desires; I can, then, in spite of my littleness, aspire to sanctity. For me to become greater is impossible; I must put up with myself just as I am with all my imperfections. But I wish to find the way to go to Heaven by a very straight, short, completely new little way. We are in a century of inventions: now one does not even have to take the trouble to climb the steps of a stairway; in the homes of the rich, an elevator replaces them nicely. I, too, would like to find an elevator to lift me up to Jesus, for I

am too little to climb the rough stairway of perfection. So I have looked in the books of the saints for a sign of the elevator I long for, and I have read these words proceeding from the mouth of eternal Wisdom: "He that is a little one, let him turn to me" (Proverbs 9:16). So I came, knowing that I had found what I was seeking, and wanting to know, O my God, what You would do with the little one who would answer Your call, and this is what I found:

"As one whom the mother caresses, so will I comfort you. You shall be carried at the breasts and upon the knees they shall caress you" (Isaiah 66:12–13). Never have more tender words come to make my soul rejoice. The elevator which must raise me to the heavens is Your arms, O Jesus! For that I do not need to grow; on the contrary, I must necessarily remain small, become smaller and smaller. O my God, You have surpassed what I expected, and I want to sing Your mercies. (Saint Thérèse of the Infant Jesus, *Histoire d'une Ame: Manuscrits Autobiographiques* [Paris: Éditions du Seuil, 1998], 244.)

Appendix 2
HOW TO DO A VERSE STUDY

A verse study is an exciting Bible study tool that can help to bring the Scriptures to life! By reading, reflecting on, and committing a verse to memory, we open ourselves to the Holy Spirit, who reveals very personal applications of our Lord's words and actions to our daily lives.

Learning to do a verse study is not difficult, but it can be demanding. In this Walking with Purpose™ study, a Bible verse has been selected to reinforce a theme of each lesson. To do the verse study, read the verse and then follow these simple instructions. You'll be on your way to a deeper and more personal understanding of Scripture.

- **Read the verse and the paragraph before and after the verse.**

- **Write out the selected verse.**

- **Paraphrase.**
  Write the verse using your own words. What does the verse say?

- **Ask questions.**
  Write down any questions you have about the verse. What does it say that you don't understand?

- **Use cross-references.**
  Look up other Bible verses that help to shed light on what the selected verse means. A study Bible will often list cross-references in the margin or in the study notes. Another excellent resource is Biblos.com. This website allows you to enter a specific Bible verse and it will provide many cross-references and additional insights into the passage of Scripture you selected. Record any insights you gain from the additional verses you are able to find.

- **Make a personal application.**
  What does the verse say to you personally? Is there a promise to make? a warning to heed? an example to follow? Ask God to help you find something from the verse that you can apply to your life.

The recommended Bible translations for use in Walking with Purpose™ studies are: The New American Bible, which is the translation used in the United States for the readings at Mass; The Revised Standard Version, Catholic Edition; and The Jerusalem Bible.

A SAMPLE VERSE STUDY

1. **Verse:**
   John 15:5   "I am the vine, you are the branches. Those who abide in me and I in them bear much fruit, because apart from me you can do nothing."

2. **Paraphrase:**
   Jesus is the vine, I am the branch. If I abide in Him, then I'll be fruitful, but if I try to do everything on my own, I'll fail at what matters most. I need Him.

3. **Questions:**
   What does it mean to abide? How does Jesus abide in me? What kind of fruit is Jesus talking about?

4. **Cross-references:**
   John 6:56   "He that eats my flesh, and drinks my blood, abides in me, and I in him." This verse brings to mind the Eucharist, and the importance of receiving Christ in the Eucharist as often as possible. This is a very important way to abide in Jesus.

   John 15:7   "If you abide in me, and my words abide in you, ask for whatever you wish, and it will be done for you." How can Jesus' words abide in me if I never read them? I need to read the Bible if I want to abide in Christ.

   John 15:16   "It was not you who chose me, but I who chose you and appointed you to go and bear fruit that will remain, so that whatever you ask the Father in my name he may give you." Not all fruit remains. Some is good only temporarily—on earth. I want my fruit to remain in eternity—to count in the long run.

   Galatians 5:22–23   "The fruit of the Spirit is love, joy, peace, patience, kindness, generosity, faithfulness, gentleness, self-control." These are some of the fruits that will be seen if I abide in Christ.

5. **Personal Application:**

   I will study my calendar this week, making note of where I spend my time. Is most of my time spent on things that will last for eternity (fruit that remains)? I'll reassess my priorities in light of what I find.

NOTES

Appendix 3
CONVERSION OF HEART

The Catholic faith is full of beautiful traditions, rituals, and sacraments. As powerful as they are, it is possible for them to become mere habits in our lives, instead of experiences that draw us close to the heart of Christ. In the words of John Paul II, they can become acts of "hollow ritualism." We might receive our first Communion and the sacraments of confession and confirmation, yet never experience the interior conversion that opens the heart to a personal relationship with God.

Pope Benedict XVI has explained that the "door of faith" is opened at one's baptism, but we are called to open it again, walk through it, and rediscover and renew our relationship with Christ and His Church.[38]

So how do we do this? How do we walk through that door of faith so we can begin to experience the abundant life that God has planned for us?

GETTING PERSONAL

The word *conversion* means "the act of turning." This means that conversion involves a turning away from one thing and a turning toward another. When you haven't experienced conversion of heart, you are turned *toward* your own desires. You are the one in charge, and you do what you feel is right and best at any given moment. You may choose to do things that are very good for other people, but the distinction is that *you are choosing*. You are deciding. You are the one in control.

Imagine driving a car. You are sitting in the driver's seat, and your hands are on the steering wheel. You've welcomed Jesus into the passenger's seat, and have listened to His comments. But whether or not you follow His directions is really up to you. You may follow them or you may not, depending on what seems right to you.

When you experience interior conversion, you decide to turn, to get out of the driver's seat, move into the passenger's seat, and invite God to be the driver. Instead of seeing Him as an advice giver or someone nice to have around for the holidays, you give Him control of every aspect of your life.

More than likely, you don't find this easy to do. This is because of the universal struggle with pride. We want to be the ones in charge. We don't like to be in

---

[38] Pope Benedict XVI, *Apostolic Letter: Porta Fidei*, for the Indiction of the Year of Faith, October 11, 2011.

desperate need. We like to be the captains of our ships, charting our own courses. As William Ernest Henley wrote, "I am the master of my fate: I am the captain of my soul."

Conversion of heart isn't possible without humility. The first step is to recognize your desperate need of a savior. Romans 6:23 states that the "wages of sin is death." When you hear this, you might be tempted to justify your behavior, or compare yourself with others. You might think to yourself, "I'm not a murderer. I'm not as bad as this or that person. If someone were to put my good deeds and bad deeds on a scale, my good ones would outweigh the bad. So surely I am good enough? Surely I don't deserve death!" When this is your line of thought, you are missing a very important truth: Just one mortal sin is enough to separate you from a holy God. Just one mortal sin is enough for you to deserve death.[39] Even your best efforts to do good fall short of what God has required in order for you to spend eternity with Him. Isaiah 64:6 says, "All our righteous acts are like filthy rags." If you come to God thinking that you are going to be accepted by Him based on your "good conduct," He will point out that your righteousness is nothing compared to His infinite holiness.

Saint Thérèse of Lisieux understood this well, and wrote, "In the evening of my life I shall appear before You with empty hands, for I do not ask You to count my works. All our justices are stained in Your eyes. I want therefore to clothe myself in Your own justice and receive from Your love the eternal possession of Yourself."[40]

She recognized that her works, her best efforts, wouldn't be enough to earn salvation. Salvation cannot be earned. It's a free gift. Saint Thérèse accepted this gift, and said that if her justices or righteous deeds were stained, then she wanted to clothe herself in Christ's own justice. We see this described in 2 Corinthians 5:21: "God made him who had no sin to be sin for us, so that in him we might become the righteousness of God."

How did God make Him who had no sin to be sin for you? This was foretold by the prophet Isaiah: "But he was pierced for our transgressions, he was crushed for our iniquities; the punishment that brought us peace was upon him, and by his wounds we are healed" (Isaiah 53:5).

---

[39] One sin was enough to merit death for the first human beings who were in the state of preternatural perfection. For us, joined to Christ in His Body, one mortal sin merits death. Venial sin does not, although venial sin makes it easier to commit mortal sin. See CCC #1854-#1864.

[40] Saint Thérèse of Lisieux, "Act of Oblation to Merciful Love," June 9, 1895.

Jesus accomplished this on the cross. Every sin committed, past, present, and future, was placed on Him. Now, *all the merits of Jesus can be yours.* He wants to fill your empty hands with His own virtues.

But first, you need to recognize, just as Saint Thérèse did, that you are little. You are weak. You fail. You need forgiveness. You need a savior.

When you come before God in prayer and acknowledge these truths, He looks at your heart. He sees your desire to trust Him, to please Him, to obey Him. He says to you, "My precious child, you don't have to pay for your sins. My Son, Jesus, has already done that for you. He suffered, so that you wouldn't have to. I want to experience a relationship of intimacy with you. I forgive you.[41] Jesus came to set you free.[42] When you open your heart to me, you become a new creation![43] The old you has gone. The new you is here. If you will stay close to me, and journey by my side, you will begin to experience a transformation that brings joy and freedom.[44] I've been waiting to pour my gifts into your soul. Beloved daughter of mine, remain confident in me. I am your loving Father. Crawl into my lap. Trust me. Love me. I will take care of everything."

This is conversion of heart. This act of faith lifts the veil from your eyes and launches you into the richest and most satisfying life. You don't have to be sitting in church to do this. Don't let a minute pass before opening your heart to God and inviting Him to come dwell within you. Let Him sit in the driver's seat. Give Him the keys to your heart. Your life will never be the same again.

---

[41] "If we acknowledge our sins, he is faithful and just and will forgive our sins and cleanse us from every wrongdoing." 1 John 1:9

[42] "So if the Son makes you free, you will be free indeed." John 8:36

[43] "So whoever is in Christ is a new creation: the old things have passed away; behold, new things have come." 2 Corinthians 5:18

[44] "I will sprinkle clean water over you to make you clean; from all your impurities and from all your idols I will cleanse you. I will give you a new heart, and a new spirit I will put within you. I will remove the heart of stone from your flesh and give you a heart of flesh." Ezekiel 36:25–26

NOTES

Appendix 4
RICK WARREN INTERVIEW

In Paul Bradshaw's interview with Rick Warren, Rick said:

People ask me, What is the purpose of life? And I respond: In a nutshell, life is preparation for eternity. We were not made to last forever, and God wants us to be with him in heaven.

One day my heart is going to stop, and that will be the end of my body—but not the end of me. I may live sixty to a hundred years on earth, but I am going to spend trillions of years in eternity. This is the warm-up act—the dress rehearsal. God wants us to practice on earth what we will do forever in eternity.

We were made by God and for God, and until you figure that out, life isn't going to make sense.

Life is a series of problems: Either you are in one now, you're just coming out of one, or you're getting ready to go into another one. The reason for this is that God is more interested in your character than your comfort. God is more interested in making your life holy than he is in making your life happy.

We can be reasonably happy here on earth, but that's not the goal of life. The goal is to grow in character, in Christ's likeness.

This past year has been the greatest year of my life but also the toughest, with my wife, Kay, getting cancer.

I used to think that life was hills and valleys—you go through a dark time, then you go to the mountaintop, back and forth. I don't believe that anymore. Rather than life being hills and valleys, I believe that it's kind of like two rails on a railroad track, and at all times you have something good and something bad in your life. No matter how good things are in your life, there is always something bad that needs to be worked on. And no matter how bad things are in your life, there is always something good you can thank God for.

You can focus on your purposes, or you can focus on your problems. If you focus on your problems, you're going into self-centeredness, which is my problem, my issues, my pain. But one of the easiest ways to get rid of pain is to get your focus off yourself and onto God and others.

We discovered quickly that in spite of the prayers of hundreds of thousands of people, God was not going to heal Kay or make it easy for her. It has been very difficult for her, and yet God has strengthened her character, given her a ministry of helping other people, given her a testimony, drawn her closer to him and to people.

You have to learn to deal with both the good and the bad of life.

Actually, sometimes learning to deal with the good is harder. For instance, this past year, all of a sudden, when [*The Purpose Driven Life*] sold fifteen million copies, it made me instantly very wealthy. It also brought a lot of notoriety that I had never had to deal with before.

I don't think God gives you money or notoriety for your own ego or for you to live a life of ease. So I began to ask God what he wanted me to do with this money, notoriety, and influence. He gave me two different passages that helped me decide what to do, 2 Corinthians 9 and Psalm 72.

First, in spite of all the money coming in, we would not change our lifestyle one bit. We made no major purchases. Second, about midway through last year, I stopped taking a salary from the church. Third, we set up foundations to fund an initiative we call the Peace Plan to plant churches, equip leaders, assist the poor, care for the sick, and educate the next generation. Fourth, I added up all that the church had paid me in the twenty-four years since I started the church, and I gave it all back. It was liberating to be able to serve God for free.

We need to ask ourselves: Am I going to live for possessions? Popularity? Am I going to be driven by pressures? Guilt? Bitterness? Materialism? Or am I going to be driven by God's purposes [for my life]?

When I get up in the morning, I sit on the side of my bed and say, God, if I don't get anything else done today, I want to know you more and love you better. God didn't put me on earth just to fulfill a to-do list. He's more interested in what I am than what I do. That's why we're called human beings, not human doings.

Happy moments, PRAISE GOD. Difficult moments, SEEK GOD. Quiet moments, WORSHIP GOD. Painful moments, TRUST GOD. Every moment, THANK GOD.

Answer Key

NOTES

Lesson 1, Day One

1. Regardless of whether the talents were in the pocket of the master or in the hands of the servant, they belonged to the master. They were to be invested on *his* behalf, and were to serve *his* purposes.

2. God knowingly distributes "talents" unequally. This difference has always been part of His plan, because He "wills that each receive what he needs from others, and that those endowed with particular 'talents' share the benefits with those who need them." (CCC 1937) When we ignore this, and when those who have been given much use what they have selfishly or lazily, orphans lack homes, people lack food, hearts starve for affection, and people spiritually die for lack of Christ.

3. The lazy servant was afraid of his master, considering him a "demanding person." Perhaps the servant felt that the master expected too much of him, or even felt resentful that he had only been given one talent when others were given more. His view of his master had a direct impact on his handling of his talent. In the same way, our view of God will have a significant impact on whether or not we serve Him wholeheartedly in this broken world. If we see Him as a demanding taskmaster, if we're afraid that He'll get angry if we fail, we'll probably not bother to try at all. If we're so busy noticing our deficits and the wonderful way He's blessed others with gifts, talents, and resources, we'll be unlikely to move out of our comfort zones to serve Him.

4. Answers will vary.

Lesson 1, Day Two

1. It could have been a trap—someone could have been pretending to be hurt in order to rob whoever stopped to help. It was personally costly; the Good Samaritan shared his own oil and wounds, and spent money on the man's care in the inn. The man's need was unexpected, unplanned. The Good Samaritan, like everyone in the past and present, had places to go and people to see. Stopping to help cost the Samaritan time, and it was probably inconvenient.

2. Both might have been on their way to an important appointment connected to their religious ministry. There could have been concern about the bloodiness of the man; anytime a Jewish person encountered blood, he had to go through a lengthy purification ritual.

3. Answers will vary.

4. Answers will vary.

Lesson 1, Day Three

1. Jesus is the vine, God the Father is the vine grower, and Christians are the branches. The primary aim of the branches should be to remain connected to the vine. This means that as a Christian, my primary objective every day should be to remain connected to Christ. This isn't something I give a little attention to on Sunday; this should be my daily focus.

2. This commandment calls us to love one another sacrificially. It's a picture of serving one another, and in doing so, bearing spiritual fruit that will last, carrying over from this life into the next.

3. Saint Teresa of Calcutta's lack of pride and abundance of humility kept her clinging to the vine, Jesus. She knew that although there were times when she felt weary and weak, God's strength was enough.
4. Answers will vary.

Lesson 1, Day Four
1. **A.** God said, "I will be with you."
   B. Answers will vary.
2. God said that Gideon had too many soldiers with him for God to deliver Midian into the Israelites' power. God wanted to make sure that the Israelites knew, beyond a shadow of a doubt, that God had brought the victory.
3. In Judges 7:4–7, the Lord had Gideon lead the ten thousand soldiers down to the water to drink. God told him to separate the men who lapped up the water like dogs from the men who knelt down to drink by raising their hands to their mouths. This brought the number of soldiers standing alongside Gideon to three hundred.
4. In verse 9, God promised Gideon that He had delivered the Midianites into his power. In verses 10–14, God strengthened Gideon's faith by guiding him to overhear a Midianite soldier's dream predicting a victory for the Israelites. The Israelites' weapons were horns, jars, and torches inside the jars. The Midianites killed each other. In the confusion and fear, they all turned on each other. Those who weren't killed fled.

Lesson 1, Day Five
1. Answers will vary.
2. In Mark 10:35–37, James and John (close friends of Jesus) were all about their egos. Their primary concern was making sure that they'd get recognition and a place of honor in Christ's kingdom. In John 14:8–9, another of Jesus' disciples, Philip, revealed how little he had understood who Jesus really was. This is a subtler pain in relationships, the feeling of being misunderstood or not known. Jesus was not immune to the feelings associated with this reality. There isn't much that's worse than being betrayed by a friend. Judas' kiss would have pierced Jesus' heart with the deepest pain. He had held nothing back from Judas, but Judas responded to Jesus' love and sacrificial giving with betrayal.
3. Focusing on "the joy that was set before Him" gave Jesus the strength to endure the cross.
4. Anytime we keep our eyes on our mission, on the end result that we are hoping God will accomplish through us, we are strengthened to persevere. When we meditate on what Jesus suffered for us, and then are reminded that we haven't yet suffered to the point of shedding blood, some of our frustrations don't seem quite so intolerable.

Lesson 2, Day One
1. If we are looking for contentment by having more money, we'll find that our tastes and desires continue to grow, keeping satisfaction just out of reach. King Solomon wrote **Ecclesiastes 2:10–11** when he was the richest man in the world. He had it all, but found that it was meaningless. Even with great riches, contentment was as elusive as the wind. **CCC 2536** says that "our thirst for another's goods is immense, infinite, never quenched. Thus it is written: 'He who loves money never has money enough.'"

2. All material wealth comes from God. Riches and glory are from Him. God owns it all, and loans it to us. In Lesson 8, we learned that we are only stewards of our time, not owners. In that same way, all that we possess is owned by God and on loan to us.

3. **A.** Answers will vary.
   B. Answers will vary.

4. Answers will vary.

Lesson 2, Day Two

1. **CCC 27**

   - The desire for God is written in the human heart, because man is created by God and for God.
   - God never ceases to draw man to Him.
   - The only place we'll find the truth and happiness that we never stop searching for is *in God.*
   - Our dignity rests on the fact that we're called to communion with God.
   - She needs to freely acknowledge that love, and entrust herself to God.

2. Both CCC 27 and Rick Warren make the point that we were created by God and for God. The only way we'll find happiness is by making our life purpose knowing God and living in such a way that we can spend eternity with Him. All other purposes, passions, and pursuits must be secondary to this primary one. Every day spent preparing for eternity is a day well spent.

3. God calls us to live a holy life. This is a key part of our life's purpose. When we live a holy life, characterized by obedience, we bring honor to God. It also benefits us, because if we ignore God's commands, we won't find the happiness and contentment that we were created for. Contentment is tied to answering God's call to be holy.

4. Answers will vary.

Lesson 2, Day Three

1. **1 Peter 5:6-7**

   - We're told to cast our worries upon God. The Greek word for cast is translated as "hurl." This is a powerful letting go or release.
   - We can confidently cast our worries on God because He cares for us. God is not distant or uncaring. He is personal, and intimately concerned and acquainted with all the details of our lives. He wants what is best for us. When we entrust our worries to Him, we're entrusting them to the One who loves us like no other.
   - We are told to humble ourselves under the mighty hand of God.

2. Answers will vary.

3. **2 Corinthians 10:4–5** The weapons are not of flesh. They are enormously powerful, capable of destroying fortresses. They can destroy the arguments and what-if scenarios that tempt us to not trust God. They help us to take every thought captive to Christ. They can break down the barriers that keep us from believing that God will take care of us.
   Ephesians 6:13–18 The weapons mentioned in this passage are righteousness (verse 14), faith (verse 16), the sword of the Spirit, which is Scripture (verse 17), and prayer.

4. Answers will vary.

Lesson 2, Day Four

1. They told Moses that they felt they would have been better off in Egypt. At least there they had food to eat! Instead of focusing on all they had just been given, they focused on what they missed and what they didn't have.
2. God said He'd send so much meat that it would come out of their noses and would become loathsome to them. He sent it in this manner because their complaining had reached a new level. This time, they rejected the Lord in their midst, asking, "Why did we ever leave Egypt?"
3. Philippians 4:19 says that God will supply all our needs.
4. Answers will vary.

Lesson 2, Day Five

1. The all-sufficiency of Christ is seen in the following phrases: the image of the invisible God (verse 15); all things were created through Him and for Him (verse 16); He is before all things (verse 17); in Him all things hold together (verse 17); He is the head of the Church (verse 18); He is the beginning (verse 18); He is to be preeminent in all things (verse 18); the fullness of God dwells in Him; He reconciled all things for God; making peace through His blood (verse 20).
2. Answers will vary.
3. Our heavenly inheritance is imperishable, undefiled, and unfading. It's kept in heaven for us.
4. Suffering and trials give us the unique opportunity to grow in faith. They act as a refiner's fire. As the fire heats up, impurities rise to the surface. We see what we need to deal with. God meets us there, and helps us to grow to a place of greater spiritual maturity.

Lesson 3, Day One

1. Answers will vary.
2. Answers will vary.
3. We read in Proverbs 31:30 that charm is deceptive and mere outer beauty is fleeting, but a woman who respects and loves God is to be praised. In 1 Peter 3:3–4 we are challenged to pursue inner beauty. So often we make the mistake of spending more time on our appearance than on cultivating a gentle and quiet inner spirit. Clearly, God is not concerned with how we look in our skinny jeans. That's not the point of balancing our cravings.
4. Our souls are longing for God. The thirst we feel won't be satiated with coffee and soda. We were created to yearn and pine for the courts of the Lord—heaven. Our hearts and flesh cry out to be connected to the One who created us. Our deepest desire is to see God. This desire will be quenched in eternity, but communion with Him here sustains us while we wait to see Him in heaven.

Lesson 3, Day Two

1. Answers will vary.

2. Saint Paul teaches that just because something isn't sinful doesn't mean it's good for us. Something good can become bad when it dominates us. When we are ruled by a desire for anything other than God, we're being enslaved by a disordered passion.

3. The power described in Ephesians 1:18–20 is resurrection power—the same power that raised Jesus from the dead. Verse 19 tells us that this surpassing, great power is available for us, for those who believe. This is what we need to focus on whenever we are tempted to say, "I can't!" Because of Christ and His gift of His own resurrection power, placed in the hearts of those who believe, we can do all that He asks of us—not because we're strong, but because *He* is strong within us.

4. Answers will vary.

Lesson 3, Day Three

1. Jesus described His food as doing the will of His Father and finishing His work.

2. Jesus told His disciples to look up and see "the fields ripe for the harvest." He was challenging them to take a look at all the people who desperately needed to hear the good news about their Savior. Stepping out and sharing that good news would be more satisfying than anything else they might pursue.

3. Jesus responded by saying that it wasn't food that was sustaining Him; it was the Word of God.

4. **Romans 8:37** "In all these things, we conquer overwhelmingly through him who loved us."

   1 Corinthians 10:13 "No trial has come to you but what is human, God is faithful and will not let you be tried beyond your strength; but with the trial he will also provide a way out, so that you may be able to bear it."

   1 Corinthians 10:23 "'Everything is lawful,' but not everything is beneficial. 'Everything is lawful,' but not everything builds up."

Lesson 3, Day Four

1. We should be fasting in order to draw closer to God and more fully live the way He is calling us to live. Losing weight shouldn't be our motive.

2. Answers will vary.

3. Answers will vary.

4. Answers will vary.

Lesson 3, Day Five

1. Answers will vary.

2. People all around the world are asking God to give them their daily bread. Is it not possible that we are the answer to their prayers? Could it be that God is tapping on our hearts, asking us to be a part of the solution to their problem of hunger? God chooses to work out His purposes through His people, flawed though we are. We are His hands and feet. We are often the way God chooses to answer another person's prayer.

3. Jesus is mysteriously hidden in the faces of the poor.

4. Answers will vary.

Lesson 4, Day One

1. God has given each of His children a spirit of power, love, and self-control.
2. We labor and struggle to do what is right, and we do this by drawing on the power that God has placed within us through the Holy Spirit.
3. We can check ourselves by seeing who gets the credit for the victory. Do we credit ourselves, or do we recognize that God equipped us for the day of battle and that the victory belongs to Him?

Lesson 4, Day Two

1. The author of Hebrews had things he really wanted to teach his readers, but they weren't mature enough to understand them. This wasn't because it was the first time they'd been taught. The problem was that they weren't applying the lessons they had previously been exposed to. They were immature, needing to be fed milk when they should have been ready for meat.
2. When people become sluggish in hearing, they will be drawn to things that ignite their curiosity. Sound doctrine won't be tolerated (it'll be perceived as boring), and people will look for teachers who tell them what they want to hear. People will seek to be entertained more than seeking truth tellers.
3. He felt they should be teachers.
4. Answers will vary.

Lesson 4, Day Three

1. She has to exercise discipline. She needs to go into strict training, and say no to pleasurable things that would get in the way of her goal. It involves self-denial. It often involves ignoring pain and pressing on in spite of it. If she exerts this effort only every once in a while, she won't achieve her goal. She has to be consistent. The discipline needed to excel in athletics is the same discipline needed to progress in the spiritual life.
2. We're exercising self-discipline so that we can receive an "imperishable crown." This is a crown that will last forever. We're running toward a reward in heaven that can never be taken away from us.
3. Answers will vary.
4. Answers will vary.

Lesson 4, Day Four

1. God said that He would rain down bread from heaven. The people were to go out every day and gather enough for the day. On the sixth day, though, they were allowed to gather twice as much as they gathered on the other days.
2. If they tried to gather extra "bread from heaven" one day to save it for the following day, they found that the next morning it had become wormy and stank.
3. The Eucharist is our daily bread. Through it, we "become what we receive." Our daily bread is also "the readings [we] hear each day in church and the hymns [we] hear and sing. All these are necessities for our pilgrimage."
4. Answers will vary.

Lesson 4, Day Five
1. Answers will vary.
2. They didn't want the commitment to follow Christ to cost them their families or their comfort. Their response to Jesus was a "Yes, but . . ." It was a conditional commitment, which fell short of what it means to follow Christ.
3. Answers will vary.
4. Answers will vary.

Lesson 5, Day One
1. **A.** Answers will vary.
   B. Answers will vary.
2. Answers will vary.
3. Jesus tells us to stop judging. He asks us to stop pointing out the splinter in our brother's eye while ignoring the sin within our own hearts. We are to focus first on our own sin (the wooden beam). Then we can see clearly to help remove the splinter from our brother's eye. Our motive behind removing the splinter should be compassion. It should come from the desire to see our brother free from the hurt of having something "stuck in his eye" rather than judging and criticizing him in hopes that he'll get his act together.
4. Jesus said that the gates of hell wouldn't prevail against the Church.

Lesson 5, Day Two
1. She saw a crowd of people gathered together. This wasn't going to be handled quietly in private—it was to be a spectacle, something interesting for all sorts of people to listen in on. They made her stand in the middle of the group, so she was surrounded by judgment and condemnation. There was no escape. One word describes how she felt: *shame.*
2. He told them that the person who was without sin should be the first to throw a stone at her. One by one, the religious leaders walked away.
3. The people behind the issues of our day feel judged. Some examples: those with same-sex attractions, who have had or are contemplating an abortion, who have experienced the pain of divorce, who use birth control. In addition, many stay-at-home moms judge moms who work full-time, and mothers who work outside the home judge stay-at-home mothers. Whenever someone is different from us, we are tempted to judge.
4. We can look for the farthest women out—the awkward, the angry, the confused, the doubting, the hurting, the broken. Who is the woman in the back pew with one foot out the door? We can listen to her. We can seek to see life from her perspective. We can ask questions instead of spouting solutions and corrections. We can admit that we struggle, too. We can smile more. We can look in people's eyes. We can stop looking at people as they are in this moment, or as they have been in their times of greatest sin and weakness, and instead see who they can become. We can look at others through grace-healed eyes, knowing that each and every person we encounter is loved by and precious to God.

Lesson 5, Day Three
1. Matthew 5:41 says that if someone asks for our help, we are to give her more than she asked for. Our standard should be going the extra mile in serving those around us. According to 1 Corinthians 10:31, our goal should be bringing glory to God. This means

that no matter what we're doing, we recognize that we are representing Him, and we want others to have a good impression of the God within us because of the way we live. Colossians 3:23 says that no matter what we do, we should do it wholeheartedly. Our motive should be pleasing God, not people. This means that we aren't looking for recognition. God's "well done, good and faithful servant" should be enough.

2. True dialogue means that we really listen to one another. We seek to understand and gain greater clarity. It means that we need to lean in close to people who are different from us. We look for the goodness within every person, and seek to connect with openness and without prejudice.

3. Colossians 4:5–6 tells us that we should look for opportunities to connect with people who believe differently than we do. Our speech should always be gracious—seasoned with salt. This means that our words should be fresh and leave people longing for more. 1 Peter 3:15 tells us to always be ready to give an explanation to anyone who asks why we are filled with hope, but to do it with gentleness and reverence.

4. Answers will vary.

Lesson 5, Day Four
1. Cultural withdrawal is not an option. Christ commanded us to go into the world and share our faith. Jesus also said this in John 17:18: "As you sent me into the world, so I sent them into the world."

2. He said men will reproach us, persecute us, and say evil things about us.

3. Answers will vary.

4. We aren't to separate ourselves from the culture in a physical sense, but we need to be careful that we don't blend in so much that we are participating in sinful behavior.

Lesson 5, Day Five
1. It has the power to renew the life and culture of fallen man. It combats and removes the error and evil that flows from the attraction to sin. The gospel purifies and elevates our morality.

2. Instead of criticizing the cultural scene, we can step into it, creating beauty within it. In his book *Culture Making*, author Andy Crouch describes the tendency of Christians to war against culture and to criticize it. He makes the point that this does not bring the desired change. Culture does not change by being condemned, critiqued, or copied. He concludes that culture is changed only by creating more of it.[45] When Christians step into the various aspects of culture and create something original and beautiful, they are "restoring the truth, goodness, and beauty that's been lost."[46]

3. As Matthew Kelly points out in his book *Rediscover Catholicism*, "Every day, the Catholic Church feeds, houses, and clothes more people, takes care of more sick people, visits more prisoners, and educates more people than any other institution on the face of the earth could ever hope to. The very essence of health care and caring for the sick emerged through the Church, through the religious orders, in direct response to the value and

---

[45] Andy Crouch, *Culture Making: Recovering Our Creative Calling* (Downers Grove, IL: InterVarsity Press, 2008), 67.

[46] Gabe Lyons, *The Next Christians: Seven Ways You Can Live the Gospel and Restore the World* (Colorado Springs: Multnomah Books, 2012), 95.

dignity that the Gospel assigns to each and every human life."[47] He continues by drawing attention to the impact the Catholic Church has had on education: "Prior to the Church's introduction of education for the common man, education was reserved only for the nobility. Almost the entire Western world is educated today because of the Church's pioneering role in universal education."[48] The Church continues to make an enormous impact on our country, our states, and our local communities. For example, in one year, the local chapter of Catholic Charities in Chicago provided 2.2 million free meals to the hungry and the needy in that area. That's 6,027 meals a day. Examples like these are found all over the country. Yet the main message everyone hears about the Catholic Church tends to center on sex scandals and our faults. Kelly concludes, "We have forgotten our story and as a result we allow the anti-Catholic segments of the media to distort our story on a daily basis."[49] Isn't it time to start talking about and focusing on the enormous amount of goodness and beauty that is found within the Church?

4. A. A defeatism that turns us into pessimists stifles boldness and zeal.
   If we start without confidence in the future victory, we've already lost half the battle and have buried our talents.

   B. We need to remember that God's grace is sufficient for us, and His power is made perfect in our weakness.

   C. Answers may vary.

---

[47] Matthew Kelly, *Rediscover Catholicism: A Spiritual Guide to Living with Passion & Purpose* (Cincinnati: Beacon Publishing, 2010), 18.
[48] Ibid.
[49] Ibid., 19.

NOTES

Prayer Pages

 NOTES

The Grail Prayer

Lord Jesus,
I give You my hands to do Your work.
I give You my feet to go Your way.
I give You my eyes to see as You do.
I give You my tongue to speak Your words.
I give You my mind that You may think in me.
I give You my spirit that You may pray in me.
Above all, I give You my heart that You may love in me
Your Father and all mankind.
I give You my whole self that You may grow in me,
So that it is You, Lord Jesus,
Who live and work and pray in me.

Prayer Requests

Date:

Date:

Prayer Requests

Date:

Date:

Prayer Requests

Date:

Date:

NOTES

NOTES

NOTES

NOTES

"For to the one who has, more will be given"
Matthew 13:12

CHRIST'S LOVE IS ENDLESS.

And the journey doesn't end here.

Walking With Purpose is more than a Bible study, it's a supportive community of women seeking lasting transformation of the heart. And you are invited.

Walking With Purpose believes that change happens in the hearts of women – and, by extension, in their families and beyond – through Bible study and community. We welcome all women, irrespective of faith background, age, or marital status.

Connect with us online for regular inspiration and to join the conversation. There you'll find insightful blog posts, Scriptures, and downloads.

For a daily dose of spiritual nourishment, join our community on Facebook, Twitter, Pinterest and Instagram.

And if you're so moved to start a Walking With Purpose study group at home or in your parish, take a look at our website for more information.

walkingwithpurpose.com
The Modern Woman's Guide to the Bible.

walking with purpose

NOTES

❋ DEEPEN YOUR FAITH ❋ OPEN YOUR ARMS ❋ ❋ BROADEN YOUR CIRCLE ❋

When your heart opens, and your love for Christ deepens, you may be moved to bring Walking With Purpose to your friends or parish. It's rewarding experience for many women who, in doing so, learn to rely on God's grace while serving Him.

If leading a group seems like a leap of faith, consider that you already have all the skills you need to share the Lord's Word:

- Personal commitment to Christ
- Desire to share the love of Christ
- Belief in the power of authentic, transparent community

The Walking With Purpose community supports you with:

- Training
- Mentoring
- Bible study materials
- Promotional materials

Few things stretch and grow our faith like stepping out of our comfort zone and asking God to work through us. Say YES, soon you'll see the mysterious and unpredictable ways He works through imperfect women devoted to Him.

Remember that if you humbly offer Him what you can, He promises to do the rest.

"See to it that no one misses the grace of God" Hebrews 12:15

Learn more about bringing Walking with Purpose to your parish. Visit us at walkingwithpurpose.com The Modern Woman's Guide To The Bible.

 NOTES

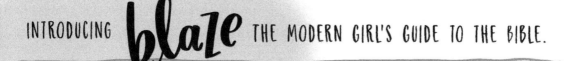
Do you want to help girls grow in confidence, faith, and kindness?

The Lord is calling for women like you to speak truth into the hearts of young girls – girls who are understandably confused about their true worth and beauty. Blaze is a fun and engaging program developed especially for 7th and 8th grade girls to counteract the cultural forces that drive them to question their value, purpose, and faith.

Like Walking With Purpose, Blaze makes the wisdom of the Bible relevant to today's challenges. Blaze teaches girls to recognize the difference between the loving, affirming voice of their heavenly Father and the voices that tell them they aren't good enough.

Would you like to be a positive influence on the girls you know? Start a Blaze program in in your parish or community.

It's easy and convenient to share God's word with a Leader's Guide and Blaze kit that includes:

- Blaze Prayer Journals
- Truth vs. Lie Cards
- Fun gifts for the girls
- Facebook and Instagram messaging to maintain connection and amplify the message

Additional resources to nurture girls' spiritual growth:

- Discovering My Purpose – a 6-session Bible study that leads girls on an exploration of their own spiritual gifts
- Between You & Me – a 40-day conversation guide for mothers and daughters

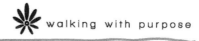
walking with purpose

For more spiritual inspiration or to learn more about Blaze and Walking With Purpose, visit us at walkingwithpurpose.com/BLAZE

You're also invited to join our community on Facebook, Twitter, Pinterest and Instagram.

"Be who God meant you to be and you will set the world on fire." - Saint Catherine of Siena

NOTES

FEARLESS & FREE
EXPERIENCING HEALING AND WHOLENESS IN CHRIST

Fear is a powerful emotion, and part of the human condition. Life isn't easy. But we were never meant to go it alone. God has wired us for connection – to Him.

Do you long to be grounded in a love that will never fail you?

Fearless and Free is for any woman confronting the reality of her fears. When suffering slams into you and leaves you reeling, or you feel great one day, and down on the mat the next, turn to this Scripture study.

Do you long for healing and wholeness? Would you like to be grounded in a love that will never fail?

In these six compassionate lessons, you'll learn to:

- **WAKEN** to the reality of who you are in Christ,

- **WRESTLE** with the battle in your mind, and conquer the enemy who seeks to steal your true identity.

- Be strengthened as a **WARRIOR** to reclaim your footing and move forward in life.

Fearless and Free is not about surviving; it's about flourishing in Christ's love, the One who truly loves you completely and without end.

**Learn more about *Fearless and Free* at walkingwithpurpose.com
The Modern Woman's Guide To The Bible.**

walking with purpose

NOTES

walking with purpose

 Mission

Walking with Purpose transforms the hearts
and lives of women by providing Bible studies
that enable women to know Christ
through Scripture and the teachings of the
Roman Catholic Church.

 Vision

To enable every Catholic woman
in America to experience our life-changing
Bible study, ***Opening Your Heart.***

Join us in transforming the hearts and lives of women.
Make a gift to Walking with Purpose today!

walkingwithpurpose.com/donate